THE

BEAUTY CARE

PAT BAIKIE

Contents

Published exclusively for
J Sainsbury Limited
Stamford Street, London SE1 9LL
by Cathay Books
59 Grosvenor Street, London W1

First published 1981

ISBN 0 86178 070 1

Printed in Hong Kong

Introduction

This is the beauty book for you if you care about your appearance but don't want to become a slave to your looks. You must admit that, taken too seriously, the whole business of beauty can become a time-consuming chore. Looking beautiful should be fun! The secret is to put minimum effort into producing maximum rewards. One way of achieving that goal is to let your natural assets and basic beauty routines work to your best advantage.

Take eating, for instance. Aim to eat for beauty and you will discover the delights of a slender figure and healthy hair, skin, eyes and nails. With positive assets like these, you can keep skin care and make-up in perspective.

Understand your skin – its type, how to treat it and get the best from it. Apply the same rule to your hair. Your skin maxim will be a minimum of maintenance, using preparations geared to your skin type. Don't expect miracles from pots and tubes – they're to make you look more attractive, not to create unnatural beauty.

Beauty is a state of mind. Obviously good bone structure, make-up and beauty aids help, but in the main beauty comes from inside – from a feeling of well-being, a zest for life. If you feel good, you will look good. Make-up is there to help you make the most of the natural beauty you have – to make you look even better. The sort of compliment you want to hear is '*you're* looking good today', and not 'your make-up is looking good today'. To complete the picture, frame it with a healthy head of hair, in a style that's right for your hair type and right for you.

The *Sainsbury Book of Beauty* provides you with all you need to know about looking good and keeping healthy.

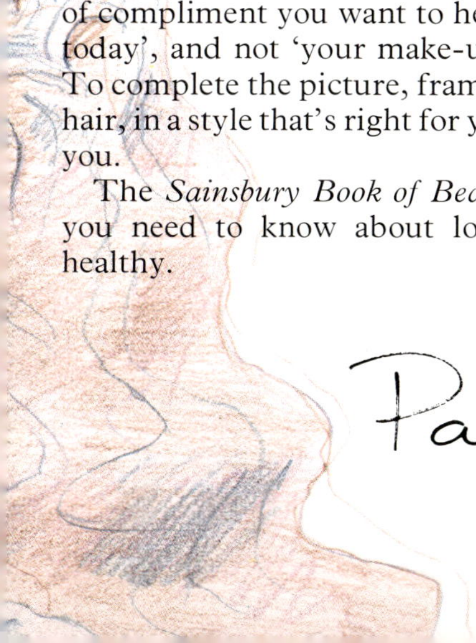

Pat Baikie

Skin Care: Face

Skin which has been looked after should be firm, yet elastic and full of glowing vitality. Maintaining that happy medium means keeping your skin scrupulously clean and balancing its care to suit every change – from the passing of years to the switch of seasons and temperatures.

Regular cleansing is tremendously important to healthy skin for we need to remove five types of dirt from our faces: perspiration, excess oil from the sebaceous glands, dust, dead cells and make-up.

Regular protection is necessary. Apart from actual bone structure, your face is made up of muscles, fat and the fluids which fill the tissues and give your face firmness and fullness. When you start to lose muscle mass or fat or fluid, wrinkles appear. This gradual loss of the skin's elasticity is a natural part of the ageing process and, although you cannot stop it, you can slow it down. A little prevention goes a long way towards warding off prematurely wrinkled skin. Proper cleansing helps, plus toning, moisturising and conditioning.

Your skin's needs vary with age. The pattern to expect is as follows. In your teens: normal/dry or oily/problem skin. In your twenties and thirties: normal/dry or oily skin. In your forties and fifties: normal/dry or dry skin. Sixties on: very dry.

From your twenties on, pay special attention to the delicate skin around the eyes – the most sensitive part of the face and especially prone to dryness and wrinkles. The throat area is vulnerable too, as is the neck – particularly prone to ageing because it has very few oil glands.

In any year, your skin may need to have its care adjusted. At home, in winter especially, both central heating and constantly varying room temperatures can make the skin feel dehydrated. This calls for more moisturising care.

Holidays at home or abroad can upset the skin. The weather, including sunlight, temperatures and humidity is generally to blame. From the skin's point of view, the most detrimental holiday climates are cold dry (mountain) air and hot dry (desert) air. In the former, you need to cleanse less frequently and apply moisturiser more often. In a hot, dry climate you are bound to perspire more which washes away the benefits of your moisturiser; you therefore need to apply it much more frequently.

Wherever the water is hard and contains chemicals, avoid soap and water cleansing; use a cleansing lotion instead.

How clean is clean enough?
No skin can ever be 100 per cent clean from one moment to the next, for the skin is constantly discharging a certain amount of sebum and perspiration to keep the moisture and oil balance within the inner skin. It's important that all the superficial debris is cleansed away regularly otherwise pores will become blocked and blemishes will start.

A really clean skin should have a uniform colour and translucency – free of debris to allow the upper layer to admit and reflect light. Since sebum flows at varying rates from different skins, an adequate cleansing routine for one skin may be far from sufficient for another. Every skin should be cleansed in the morning to remove the dead skin and oils discharged during the night, then again at bedtime and every time fresh make-up is applied. Frequency depends on the skin type; oily skin may need four or five cleansings a day.

Toning up
Tone or freshen your skin after you've cleansed it; this is an extension of cleansing. Choose an astringent lotion, skin freshener or toner: all help remove traces of make-up or oil from your skin. Most fresheners tighten the pores temporarily and stimulate circulation.

Adding moisture

Every type of skin needs a moisturiser to help retard the evaporation of natural moisture. Don't confuse the loss of moisture with the loss of oils; they are two different processes. Oily skins can lose moisture as well as oil and there are lightweight moisturisers for them. For oil-starved skins, there are heavier moisturisers which often add lubrication as well as moisture to help retain liquid in the skin.

Moisturising is an important part of any beauty routine, summer or winter. Your face is constantly exposed to elements which dry out the skin – sun, wind and cold weather, for example. Central heating creates a very dry atmosphere which can really upset natural moisture levels in the skin.

Your skin care routine

Normal skin: If you are fortunate enough to have normal skin, help keep it that way by using a cream or creamy lotion to cleanse it. At night follow this by washing your face with a mild soap. Tone your skin after cleansing with a non-drying skin freshener. Use a moisturiser at bedtime and under make-up – especially when the humidity is low.

Dry skin: Remove make-up at night with two applications of cream or a creamy lotion especially formulated for dry skin. You might also want to wash your face with a mild soap. Next step: tone your skin with a non-drying skin freshener. Since your skin needs plenty of lubrication, use an extra-rich cream at night, paying special attention to your throat and the area around your eyes. In the morning, wash with a gentle lather or – if you have very dry skin – rinse your face with warm water. Use a thin film of moisturiser under make-up at all times.

Oily skin: Wash with a cleanser – preferably medicated – in warm water at least three times a day; use a soap, liquid or gel cleanser. Massage with your fingertips, giving special attention to the forehead, nose, chin and hairline. Rinse off suds with warm water. Follow with a cold water rinse and pat dry. Sponge your face with cotton wool moistened with astringent or a non-oily medicated lotion.

Blackheads are usually associated with oily skin; they are caused by congestion below the surface. For treatment, see Skin problems (page 16).

Combination skin: If your skin is dry at the sides and oily down the middle, treat these areas separately – using dry skin preparations on outer areas and an oily-skin routine for the middle portion. It is perfectly possible to wash the oily part of your face more frequently than the dry areas. Massage cleanser on oily parts and rinse off with water using your cupped hand or a beaker.

LEFT: *Face massage step 3. Making gentle circular movements on the end of the chin with the middle fingers of each hand.*

ABOVE LEFT: *Then working the fingers around the mouth towards the nose.*
ABOVE: *Smoothing fingers lightly over the cheekbones.*

Massage is 'exercise'

Massage, if performed correctly, brings a fresh supply of blood to the skin's surface, helps clear away impurities, feeds the tissues and tones up tired muscles. Aim to massage your skin once a week. You can use soap suds, moisturiser or a conditioning night cream. Massage for 5 minutes at a time. Always begin on the lower part of the face – working the cream or soap until it is soft and warm. Use six movements – all upward and outward – avoiding the area around the eyes. **1.** Place left hand at the base of the throat and, with a firm circular movement, work up the right side of the neck towards the chin. Repeat, using the right hand up the left side of the neck. **2.** With the backs of the hands slap briskly beneath the chin – one hand and then the other. Shake hands to prevent stiffness. **3.** Place middle fingers of each hand on the point of the chin and make circular movements, working up round the mouth and in towards the nose. Smooth out lightly over the cheekbones. **4.** Place middle fingers of one hand and then the other over cheek. Stroke briskly upwards using alternate hands. Repeat on the other side of your face. **5.** Using both hands stroke up the centre of the nose between eyebrows and smooth out over brow towards the temples. **6.** Then knuckle into the brow with rotary movements using alternate hands.

Handle with care
Care for your skin by handling it gently. Soaps, cleansing lotions and creams, moisturisers and conditioning creams should all be applied to the skin as gently as possible; otherwise you defeat the object of the application – which is to maintain youthful, supple and firm skin.

Never scrub or drag at your face. If you suspect that you are being heavy-handed, 'handicap' yourself. Instead of scooping up dollops of cream on your fingertips (wasteful, apart from anything else), use the middle finger only of each hand and learn to fingerprint products over the face instead of smearing them on indiscriminately.

Over the cheeks: When making-up, never try to apply cheek colour to a 'naked' skin. Moisturiser is a must if the colour is to go on smoothly and effectively.

RIGHT: *When you're wiping off cleansing cream or lotion, use a tissue to its best advantage. Instead of wasting several tissues – scrunching them up, one after another, and rubbing away at your face, try this.*

Wrap a tissue round your hand and fold over at the top to make a 'glove'. Wipe the tissue gently over the face. When one side is soiled, move the glove round to the clean side, then turn it inside out. Used in this way, one tissue can make a really smooth job of cleaning your face and help keep the texture firm at the same time.

Another tip – for quick, easy and gentle application of cleanser or freshener – make your own moist pads. Simply cut out circles of lint, pack them into a pretty, airtight jar and add enough of the product of your choice to saturate the 'circles'.

Around the eyes: When applying moisturiser or cream to the delicate skin beneath the eyes, use the middle or fourth finger of each hand. Look upwards and fingerprint the product on. Work outwards over the eyelids towards the outer corners, then inwards towards the nose. Finish with a series of small circular movements at the outer corner of each eye. If you are applying a camouflage product to dark circles or bags under the eyes, dot on the product and leave for a minute or two, until the warmth of the skin softens up the consistency; then blend it in with the fingertip. Alternatively, apply and blend with a brush.

On the neckline: When applying moisturiser or cream to the throat area, make sure that every single movement is upward and outward; this way you are lifting and firming the contours all the time.

Signs of the teens, twenties, thirties, forties . . . Knowing how skin changes with age and being aware of the danger areas will help you work out your own individual skin conditioning routine. For this there are day and night moisturisers, conditioning creams for general facial application and, more specifically, for the areas around eyes and throat, and face masks.

Late-teens – early-twenties: A normal skin is smooth, soft and firm, with a clear, healthy colour. It can be compared with the unblemished, polished skin of an apple. Even at this age moisturising is important, as the natural moisture cells begin to deflate.

Mid-twenties: The ideal skin resembles that of a peach – more soft and smooth, less 'glowy' than an apple. Moisturiser helps counteract the appearance of fine expression lines around the eyes.

Mid-thirties: The average skin tends to become drier, loosing some of its elasticity and fresh colouring. The main areas to watch are around eyes and mouth. Fine criss-cross lines indicate dryness and really dry patches on cheeks or forehead show up reddish in colour. Remember: laughter is not the only emotion your face registers. You could also develop your share of frown and disapproval lines. The best

The skin around the eyes gives our age away more obviously than we like to think. Perhaps laughter is to blame, but try to keep lines and wrinkles at bay with gentle products and gentle handling of the skin.

defence is massage. At this age switch to richer day and night moisturisers and stimulate the skin with massage and moisturisers.

Early forties: Watch out for deepening of under-the-eye lines and a tendency for the neck to become drier. Continue the skin care pattern of the thirties and think in terms of 24-hour nourishment. Choose moisture-based make-up ranges and eye and neck creams.

Mid-forties and on: Without a good skin care routine, your skin will become extra dry and lax, with deeply etched lines around the mouth and eyes and on the forehead. Your skin could lose its natural colour and tiny surface capillaries could rupture, leaving small, purple-red blotches. Lax muscles can make the jaw-line heavier and the corners of the mouth might droop. The neck becomes more lined and the throat muscles sag a little. Gentle massage with appropriate creams can give good results in all these vulnerable areas. And remember that skin care need not only be a bedtime routine.

Skin problems

Allergies: If your complexion seems constantly itchy, chapped or very rough, you may be allergic to certain foods or cosmetics. Your doctor and/or a dermatologist can usually help you track down the cause. If cosmetics are the problem, you can minimise irritations by using hypo-allergenic creams and make-up. If in spite of that you still think a cosmetic you are using has triggered off a reaction, try to consider whether it is just an intolerance or insensitivity – a feeling of discomfort (eg wrong consistency) – rather than a real allergy.

Try a patch test. Dab the product on the inside of your wrist and wait 24 hours. If reddening or swelling occurs, you are probably allergic to an ingredient in the product and should stop using it.

Cosmetic ingredients that can damage the skin are either primary irritants or sensitisers. Primary irritants disturb the skin soon after application so they can be easily identified and avoided. However the allergic reaction to a sensitiser takes longer to develop – perhaps after weeks or months of trouble-free wearing of a product.

When you suspect you're allergic to something, write direct to the manufacturer concerned, returning the product and giving as much information as possible along the following lines. State when you used the product and whether you had used it before; describe the reaction, where it appeared and how soon after application; mention also any history of skin trouble. Manufacturers generally pass on complaints to the company chemist and/or consultant dermatologist who should come back with a satisfactory reply and alternative product suggestions. Most allergy complaints are resolved.

Blemishes: Minor skin problems can turn into more serious ones if they are not dealt with properly. If blemishes (blackheads and spots) persist in spite of careful skin care and good health, you should see your doctor. Blackheads are generally associated with oily skin and are caused by congestion below the skin's surface. Sebum in the skin becomes irritated by bacteria and a blockage occurs; when the head of the blockage meets the air it turns black, giving the blemishes their characteristic appearance.

Cleansing alone will not remove blackheads. Try softening them with hot compresses, then ease them out with a comedo extractor. This is a spoon-shaped instrument with a hole in the bowl through which you ease the blackhead or comedo – the medical term. If the number of blackheads increases, this may be a sign that oily skin is not getting clean enough and oil is building up to clog pores. Cleaning your face more often may help to prevent this build up.

Acne: This is a common complaint, especially among teenagers. Acne is the result of a disturbance in the activity of the sebaceous glands – glands in the deeper layers of the skin which secrete fatty matter. While the exact cause of the disturbance is not known, both hormone imbalance and local bacterial infections seem to play a part in its development. Doctors suggest that emotional stress, fatigue, nervous tension, improper facial hygiene and certain foods, drugs and cosmetics tend to produce flare-ups of acne – though they are not causes. Acne can also be hereditary.

Although acne cannot be prevented, it can often be controlled once it appears, by following this daily treatment. First scrub your hands, then cleanse your face with a medicated soap, sudsy liquid or gel. Using your fingertips, gently massage lather all over face for a few minutes. Rinse with hot water, then with cool water. Do this three times a day, more often if you can.

If you see a pimple starting, apply a solution of equal parts of antiseptic lotion and water on a bit of cotton wool. Change to a fresh piece of cotton wool every 5 minutes and continue the application for about 30 minutes. Do this twice a day, after thorough cleansing. At bedtime and under make-up, you could apply medication, in the form of a flesh-tinted cream or invisible gel.

In addition to following this skin care routine, you should drink plenty of water and try not to become constipated. Wear an off-the-face hair-do to keep scalp oils and dandruff from drifting onto your face, and use a medicated shampoo often. If your skin problem is serious enough to require a doctor's care, he will probably give you a list of foods to avoid and procedures to follow.

Skin Care: Body

The bath or shower is the best place for a beauty bonanza, taking in skin care over all. In the shower or bath, apart from cleaning your skin, you can do all the pumicing that's necessary. Water-softened hair is easier to shave and the warmth of the water makes the skin more receptive to lubrication. The lazy approach to achieving a good skin tone is to add a moisturising product to your bath or to use a body shampoo in the shower. If you don't add a skin softener to the bath water, then apply a good moisturiser-replacement lotion after a bath. Massage in the product until it disappears, not forgetting hands and feet. During or after a bath or shower treat specific problems.

Tiny pimples: Especially noticeable on the legs, but affecting arms and bottom as well, tiny hard spots are the direct result of bad circulation. The best cure is a daily circulation booster treatment in the form of massage. In your bath or shower, use a loofah, coarse bath mitt, pumice stone or stiff circulation brush and a good lathering soap. This treatment also helps remove dead cells. Then lubricate, using a good nourishing cream. Knuckle it in – working up from the ankles, all round the calves and thighs. Then smooth in hand and body lotion, until it is completely absorbed.

Rough, dry, scaly skin: This is usually most noticeable on the legs and is often the direct result of exposure to more extreme weather conditions. The ideal solution is to soak in a warm bath to which a few drops of oil have been added. Wash with a vegetable oil soap or use a bath additive instead of soap. When you use soap, make sure that it is rinsed off completely; soap residue can cause scaling. Dry yourself thoroughly, using a friction movement. Then massage the affected parts with a concentrated body oil.

Wrinkles: These always appear first on the face and hands, parts that are constantly exposed to the elements. Knees, armpits and between the breasts are also susceptible. Elbows wrinkle too, because of leaning pressures which dry the skin.

The gradual loss of the skin's elasticity which results in wrinkles is a natural part of the ageing process; unfortunately fair skin seems to age more quickly. You cannot stop wrinkles appearing but you can slow down the ageing process. After bathing and drying thoroughly, apply a body moisturising lotion, paying particular attention to the elbows and knees. Choose a body lotion to suit your skin type.

A MOCK SAUNA: *Use two large towels and ½–1 cupful of herbs; mint and chamomile blend well. Tie the herbs in one or two muslin bags.*

Make sure the windows and doors are tightly shut, then run the hottest water you can bear into the bottom of the bath; suspend the herb bag under the pressure of the tap – to free the fragrance.

Soak the towels in the fragrant water and wring them out. Run more hot water and get up a good steam. Now wrap yourself, mummy-style, in the hot towels and sit on the edge of the bath. When the towels cool off, remove them and relax in a heated room.

Bathing routines

A sauna bath: Sauna baths are becoming more popular. The first effect of a sauna is complete relaxation of body and mind. Through a lowering of blood pressure, mental strain often disappears and the muscles relax. The usual pattern is shower, sauna, shower, sauna and relax. According to the method of heating and the degree of humidity, the sauna can be a steam bath or a dry-heat bath. Perspiration usually starts after about 8 minutes, during the first sauna. After 10 to 20 minutes in the sauna, you take a quick shower, starting warm and getting gradually cooler. You then repeat the sauna session. Perspiration breaks out very quickly the second time. After this, you take a cold shower and then relax for at least 30 minutes.

By encouraging perspiration, a sauna helps to eliminate toxins and surplus waste from the tissues. Because of the water loss, you may experience a temporary weight loss after a sauna; this will disappear as soon as you eat and drink. Never stay in a sauna too long; this can cause over-fatigue and even fainting. Try a soothing mock sauna at home (see opposite.)

A relaxing daily bath: Aim to have a daily tepid bath (31–32°C/85–90°F), or a warm one (38°C/98–101°F). Soak for 10 minutes or so and blot yourself dry; don't rub your skin. Choose bath additives for their relaxing properties or make up your own herbal sachet, using dried herbs. Infuse by putting the herbs in a muslin bag and tying it to the hot tap so the water runs through the bag. A herbal bath soothes the nervous system, nourishes the skin and should include flowers as well as leaves. Two of the most relaxing and soothing herbs are lavender and marjoram.

A quickie bath: With only 10 minutes to spare before you must begin dressing again, run tepid water into the bath. Stretch out for 5 minutes, a wet face cloth over your eyes. Then scrub all over with a loofah and rinse off. Turn the shower attachment on you – as cold as you can take it. Rinse with tepid water. Towel-dry briskly to stimulate the circulation. Double the benefits of a quickie bath by using one of the bath salt preparations which contain mineral salts.

A speedy shower: The best value top-to-toe beauty treatment is to wash everything from hair down to toes in one easy session. Wash your hair in the shower and it becomes strictly a non-chore: no ricks in your neck, no damp necklines. With a couple of minutes to spare while hair conditioner 'takes', get busy with a loofah or sponge; go clockwise round your tummy to encourage the blood's circulation and keep your waistline trim. Rinse all over in tepid water, then give yourself a good rub with a coarse towel.

Always apply anti-perspirant deodorant first thing in the morning after washing. Make sure that you've rinsed off all soap traces; any residue can interfere with the remedial action.

Personal freshness

Personal freshness means more than a daily bath and a lavish use of fragrance. The real problem of overall personal freshness is that of dealing with body odour which emanates from the armpits in particular. Everybody perspires. There are approximately two million sweat glands all over the body. These work continuously even when no noticeable moisture is present. Perspiration is an important and necessary function of the body. Firstly, it helps your system to get rid of waste products. Secondly, as perspiration evaporates, it helps maintain normal body temperature by cooling your skin. Thirdly, because it is natural body moisture, it helps keep your skin smooth and pliable.

Odour only builds up when perspiration is in contact with the bacteria in the air for any length of time. Our faces perspire too, of course, but perspiration there is removed by relatively frequent cleansing. Obviously it is not possible to remove clothes and wash underarms with soap and water as often during the day. A deodorant is designed to counteract the odour of perspiration; an anti-perspirant is designed to inhibit the flow but it also contains deodorant properties. It makes sense to use one of the dual effect preparations.

Those who are anti anti-perspirants, either because they firmly maintain that 'sweating is natural', or because they believe that sealing off a few square inches stops the skin breathing, simply end up with damp stains on close-fitting sweaters and dresses. Total 100 per cent reduction of sweat is just not possible but anti-perspirants can reduce sweating considerably – certainly enough for comfort and to prevent clothes being marked.

Choosing your deodorant/anti-perspirant: Settle for a good functional aerosol, roll-on or cream. Roll-on anti-perspirant/deodorants are available in emulsion form and in a clear liquid which dries quickly and is less sticky. Whichever you choose, use it regularly – every 24 hours on average – and let the application set before attempting to dress. Aerosol sprays dry instantly; roll-ons and creams take longer. Most formulae are not water-fast and should be re-applied after a bath or swim.

Under-arm hair should be removed regularly as it can inhibit the effectiveness of an anti-perspirant deodorant. But what about the advisability of applying odour protection after hair removal? Most product instructions suggest waiting a few hours. An immediate post-shaving remedy is the application of a finely-milled deodorant talc.

A smooth finish

There are different ways of removing unwanted hair. Which works best for you is usually a matter of trial and error.

Electrolysis: This is the only permanent way of removing hair; the roots are killed by a small electric current passing through a fine needle. You relax in a chair while the operator treats the hairs. Fine hairs which have never been tampered with may disappear in one go, but most hairs reappear and need several treatments. Discomfort during treatment can be anything from a slight tingle to a short, sharp pain, depending on the sensitivity of your skin and the operator's skill.

Waxing: This treatment is effective for 3 to 6 weeks. Waxing rips out hair at the roots, with a double bonus: no dark shadow remains and regrowth is not usually stubbly. Many people avoid this method, not liking the thought of applying hot, wax and then ripping it off! In fact, the wax need only be warm; there are even cold applications for home use.

It's always advisable to have a salon wax first: partly because you study the expert's technique, partly because regrowth is consequently weaker and easier for you to deal with. Be prepared for post-wax tingle, especially in areas where strips have overlapped. Skin can also be tender and pink, so allow at least a day between waxing and a special occasion, or sunning.

Shaving: This technique cuts the hair across at skin level and stubble grows again quickly – in 1 to 4 days. You can 'wet' shave or use an electric razor. Ladies' razors are scaled to perform well under arms and around knees. With an electric razor, apply a pre-shave lotion first, or talcum powder which dries the skin thoroughly – to give a close shave. To wet shave, use warm water and soap (not shaving cream – the skin is too soft for that).

Depilatories: These chemical hair-removers, in cream, lotion or mousse consistency, give a smoother effect than shaving, with slightly longer-lasting results. For application, see below.

Tweezing: This lasts for 1 to 4 days and is fine for isolated hairs and eyebrows; it's not advisable for patches of hair. A disadvantage is that when a hair is pulled it often splits at the root and, with the next growth, two hairs appear in place of one. Tweezers come in ordinary-grip and scissor-grip styles with three types of tip: straight-across, diagonal and spoon-shaped. The straight-across tweezers seem to take a firmer hold on the hair; the diagonal ones cope better with obstinate stubble. Never pluck hairs growing from moles.

Bleaching: This technique is effective for up to 4 weeks and minimises the appearance of hair. A patch test is advisable.

LEFT: *Applying a depilatory. Always follow manufacturer's directions, which are generally along the following lines. Clean area with warm water, no soap. Apply depilatory with a spatula to a thickness of one-eighth of an inch; leave on for the recommended time. Try stroking first against the lie of the hairs, then with them. Most users wipe off the first application with a damp cloth and re-apply blobs of depilatory to stubborn hairs; after 2 to 3 minutes, these usually come away.*

First hand impressions

Of all beauty routines, the care of hands and feet has become the chore. This is a great pity when you think of the rewards, in terms of both comfort and appeal; the hands appeal to two senses – sight and touch. In some ways, hands are noticed as much as – and handled more than – faces; we wave goodbye, we shake hands with each other, we hold hands – and so on.

To keep hands supple: Spend a minute on massage at least once a day. Keep hands upright while working in the cream – to increase the blood flow from the fingers. Swivel the thumb on each hand, working in a dab of cream to each knuckle in turn; this helps enlarged knuckles and breaks down acid deposits. To loosen up fingers, massage the entire length of each finger in turn, from the base to the tip using the thumb and first finger of each hand (see above).

LEFT: *Removing 'old' polish before a manicure. Proceed as follows. Put a little remover in the middle of a swab of cotton wool. Then press the swab to the nail of the little finger. Wait a second or two and the polish will 'lift' cleanly away. Move on to the second nail and continue until you reach the thumb. Working from the smallest to the largest nail prevents smudging.*

LEFT: *Shaping nails. Use a long emery board rather than a metal nail file, it is more pliable and less likely to shred the nail. Never file away the sides or deep into the corners or you will damage the nail. Always file from side to centre.*
OPPOSITE PAGE: *Massaging fingers using the thumb and first finger of each hand.*

One of the best quick exercises to promote hand circulation is as follows: press and rub the hands vigorously from right to left, while rotating the wrists.

Caring for your nails: A nail takes approximately 16 weeks to grow from root to tip, so miraculous overnight cures for nails cannot happen. The best policy is to aim for trouble-free nails always – by manicuring 'little and often'. Always remove 'old' polish before a manicure (see above).

Weekly manicure routine: 1. File nails to a nice oval. **2.** Massage in cuticle cream. **3.** Soak nails for a few minutes in warm soapy water. **4.** Scrub gently with a nail-brush to remove dirt. **5.** Gently push back cuticles using a cuticle pusher, rubber end hoof stick or a manicure stick with the tip wrapped in a tiny piece of cotton wool. **6.** Apply nail varnish, if liked (see page 29).

Foot-notes

Ill-fitting shoes are the cause of most foot problems; they can also be responsible for a bad back or poor posture. Corns, callouses and other localised thickenings of the skin are caused by pressure and friction which definitely start at shoe-level.

A well-fitting shoe should be half an inch longer than your foot and allow plenty of room for your toes to move. And the right size of tights or stockings is just as important; anything too small will cramp the foot and could cause, in the long run, bunions and hammer toes. When you are on holiday, give your feet as much rest from shoes as you can, and at other times walk barefoot around the house.

Bathing your feet: Aim to do this daily. Use warm, not hot water, and never steep your feet for too long – or you will dry out all the natural oils in the skin. When your feet are feeling 'achey', bathe them first in warm water, then in cold. Always dry your feet thoroughly, especially between the toes; moist skin can crack and this is how infections start.

Massaging: Using any left-over body lotion or moisturiser, or a special foot balm, massage your feet after every bath or shower. Massage in an upward direction, from toes to ankles, to stimulate the circulation. When your feet ache and there isn't time for a cold plunge, rub them briskly with cologne. If perspiration is a problem, spray on an anti-perspirant deodorant for feet; or splash on astringent, let it dry then dust your feet with talc.

Exercising your feet: At the end of the day, when you want to sit and relax, is a good time for this routine. Sit comfortably with your feet up on a chair and proceed:

1. Clench your toes, then relax them; do this six times. 2. Stretch your toes and ankles, then 'pull them back' as far as you can – feel your heels pulling really hard. Do this six times. 3. Draw circles in the air, moving the feet from the ankles; first one, then the other – six times clockwise each foot, six times anti-clockwise. 4. Cross your feet, contract your calf and thigh muscles hard, then relax them. Do this six times. Then cross your feet the other way and repeat six times.

Pedicure: Aim to give yourself a pedicure once a fortnight.

1. Soak your feet in warm soapy water, while you bathe or shower. 2. Dry feet well, especially between the toes. 3. Smooth rough spots by rubbing them gently with a pumice stone or abrasive lotion. 4. Clip nails straight across using nail scissors or nail clippers. 5. File edges smooth; don't file down into the sides of the nail because this encourages ingrown toenails. 6. Push back cuticles using a cuticle pusher or rubber end hoof stick, or an orange stick with the tip wrapped in cotton wool. 7. Apply nail polish if liked (see opposite).

1. *Before applying nail polish make sure your nails are clean and soap-free. Wipe them over with remover.* 2. *Brush on a base coat for smoothness and nail protection.* 3. *Apply two coats of polish, using three strokes; brush down the centre of the nail first, then down each side. Wipe off a hairline of polish from each nail tip. Allow nails to dry for 5 minutes between each coat.* 4. *Brush a colourless sealing coat over the nail and under the tip.* 5. *Take off traces of polish on hands or feet with cotton wool soaked in remover. Separating toes with cotton wool blobs help to prevent smudging.*

A tan can take its toll

Apart from turning you brown, the sun can dry your skin and make it look older than it should be. Ideally, aim to get the colour right without ruining your skin. To achieve this tan sensibly, using adequate protection. You should also pre-condition your skin before going into the sun and always wear moisturiser – separately or as an integral part of a sun screen. If you apply ordinary make-up on sunny days, choose brands which contain sun filters. Equally important, never neglect after-sun care. All these points are vital if you don't want your skin to show signs of ageing before it should.

When normal skin is exposed to strong sunlight, it reacts very rapidly by turning red and eventually brown. What happens is that the melanin-pigment granules under the surface of the skin – are triggered off by the sun and migrate upwards. The ultimate depth of your tan depends on the amount of pigment your skin can produce. You will also reach a stage when your pigment is fully developed and you cannot then go any darker. With subsequent reasonable exposure, you can keep the colour topped up – that's all.

Care must be taken during the first few days of sunning. If you overdo this stage of acclimatization you risk getting sun-burned, and, in the long term getting toughened, and dried-out skin. Some people also make the mistake of not accepting their maximum tan and trying to achieve darker shades.

Actual sunburn is fairly superficial. Although it is painful it doesn't leave scars; only very occasionally, a few tiny broken veins may appear especially on cheeks and around nostrils. As far as ageing the skin is concerned, the sun is much more insidious. Remember that there are rays of two sorts: infra-red ones which provide heat, and ultra-violet rays in two strengths – long rays which don't do any harm, and short ones which do. For instance, if you expose yourself endlessly to the sun, ultra-violet will eventually penetrate through to the lower layers of the skin. This results in a break-up of those elastic tissues which keep the skin supple and youthful.

Equally harmful is moisture loss. When you have been swimming, especially in sea water, don't just dry off in the heat of the sun. Always towel yourself dry. Otherwise water left on the skin evaporates and that action has a magnetic effect, drawing out even more moisture from within the deeper layers of the skin itself.

In a nutshell, there's nothing like a tan for making you feel and look on top of the world, for a tan hides skin blemishes and contrasts well with teeth and the whites of the eyes. The way to avoid the pitfalls of tanning is to apply appropriate protection both during and after sunbathing.

Make-up

Beauty is said to be in the eye of the beholder – and that's you, every time you look at yourself in the mirror and apply make-up. But there's more to making-up than meets the eye. How you see yourself and how you will appear to others can be quite different. Here's how to be sure of looking your best from any angle and in any situation.

Light up your looks: Always make-up in a light as near as possible to the light you are going to be seen in. For best daytime effect, your mirror should be backed up against the window which gets the best daylight; this way the light comes straight over the top of the mirror and on to your face. The Victorians and the Edwardians got it just right; that's why the 'ugly' backs of their dressing tables so often conspicuously occupied one of the front windows. If you want to avoid this situation, settle instead for a pretty table and a separate mirror.

To make-up for night time you ideally need about 250 watts lighting. It is best to have lighting along the sides and over the top of your mirror. If possible, position your table near a wall or ceiling light; a swivel spotlight is ideal, because you can direct the light over the top of the mirror – and place a table light either side of the mirror. If there's not much space, little half-shaded lamps are fine; turn the half shade to expose the light when you need it.

The minimum to do the maximum: This is the secret of a good make-up. Choose subtle consistencies and colours which don't conceal but simply highlight your natural good looks. It doesn't necessarily follow that the more natural the effect you are aiming for, the fewer products you need to use. You can use several and your face will keep the secret as long as you resolve to apply each product carefully, in a good light. And remember, the secret is to make-up – not patch up. In other words, be enthusiastic about make-up or leave it alone. Don't dab on little bits here and there. Patches of eye shadow on otherwise naked eyes, lipstick on a colourless face or blusher on a bare skin will only accentuate those areas of your face that are not made up.

Never make the mistake of slapping on foundation and nothing else in the forlorn hope that as long as you blot out the odd spot or blemish, you will get by without any other make-up. You won't. Foundation on its own looks flat and is very noticeable. It is worse than wearing no make-up at all.

Making up in your teens and twenties

Moisturiser is essential; ideally use a tinted one for a pretty, glowing 'canvas' which provides minimum coverage but maximum protection. Consider the best shades for your eye make-up. Brown is the most natural of all, with grey a close second. These colours may sound limiting but between the two there's a whole new colour spectrum you probably haven't investigated before: everything from soft freckle-browns to lovely deep, plummy mauve-greys. Most medium to olive skins already contain these pigments anyway, which is what makes them 'natural', but the tones are right for everyone, even a fair-skinned blonde. Ideally, blusher and lipstick should tone with eye make-up.

The bonus of linking complementary shades is that one product will very often do the work of two, or three. Take a brown eye pencil, for instance. Obviously, it's great for tidying up the shape of the eyebrows and – as long as the consistency is soft enough – for outlining eyes and lips too. Follow that with a brown eye shadow in the same tone as the pencil: blend over the eyelids, then fluff it on as a face shader.

An alternative approach to eye make-up is to use one powder eye shadow and apply it wet and dry for different effects. You'll need two brushes, of course. Use one to apply the shadow wet – as an eye liner; the consistency goes on two or three shades darker than it appears in the palette. Use the second brush to apply the shadow dry, as usual, over the eyelids. Then take a pink-tawny tone eye shadow and use that as a highlighter high on the lids under the eyebrows. The colour can also double up as a cheek blusher. This pink-tawny shade is just right for a blonde with blue eyes or a brunette with blue, grey or hazel eyes. If you have auburn hair, you need a more definite tawny shade.

So with three products, plus moisturiser, you can achieve a pretty flattering make-up. All that is missing is mascara; this is a must and, to go with this colour scheme, choose a dark brown one. Never let mascara give itself away by allowing the lashes to stick together so they become stiff and spiky. The secret is to use a wet brush or wand for application and a dry brush to take off any excess and to spread the lashes.

Finally, don't forget lipstick. A tinted lip gloss is the ideal consistency to team with a tinted moisturiser face base; keep heavier, deeper lipstick colours and textures for times when you are wearing a full make-up. Outline the lips first, then fill in with lip gloss. You really do get the most natural effect with a thin outline of dark colour filled in with a more translucent lip gloss. Here, a lovely old-rose pink tones in beautifully with the pinky-brick colour of the eye highlighter and blusher.

LEFT: *Without make-up.* ABOVE: *After applying the minimum make-up for maximum effect. First thing in the morning, apply tinted moisturiser then eye make-up. Here a brown eye pencil is used for eye liner, eyebrow pencil and lip liner; brown mascara is brushed onto the lashes. Apply, then carry with you, two eye shadows, to reinforce cheek and eye colour. And lip gloss to give lips a lovely smooth sheen.*

Making up in your thirties and forties

All women, over a certain age, should wear a tinted foundation over moisturiser. Foundation not only helps even out a blotchy skin tone, it also acts as a 'canvas' for the rest of the make-up. Powder comes into its own now too, both the loose variety, to set foundation, and a compact of pressed powder for touching up during the day. Both should be colourless – usually called translucent. The golden rule is to match your foundation to your skin tone. Use powder as an invisible topping. It's folly to think you can blot out mistakes in foundation choice by dusting on lashings of coloured powder.

Around the age of forty, eyes start to need definition rather than heavy make-up. It is very important to keep eyebrows neat and tidy; regular tweezing is necessary. The rule is that the brow should start directly above the inner corner of the eye and stop at the point where a pencil slanted from the side of your nose past the outer corner of your eye meets the brow. Make sure the outer end of your brow is as high as the starting point and check that the highest point of the curve is immediately above the iris. If you are thinning the whole arch, always pluck from underneath, never above.

With definition in mind, you need a grey or brown pencil to outline eyelids, to help make lashes look thicker. Start at the top and draw a fine line, keeping as close to the base of the lashes as you can. You might find it easier to transfer the colour to a fine brush which can edge in really close to the lashes. Define under the eyes too, but not too much – just at the outer corners and in slightly, about one third of the way along; then blur the line with the fingertip.

Take an eye shadow, in much the same colour tone as the pencil. Use it to ring the crease of the eyelid, where the eyebrow bone meets the lid, and right round under the outer corner of the eye. Blur the line until it's hardly noticeable, then introduce the first vestige of real colour. Remember that browns and greys are for definition only. Use one shadow on the actual lid; another, if you like, as a highlighter right under the eyebrow. Be sure to blend in the colours where they meet, so there are no harsh outlines.

Mascara is the next step. Apply one coat sparingly with a moist applicator, then brush the lashes through using a dry brush.

Fluff blusher on cheeks and, with what's left on the brush, apply a touch of colour high up on the sides of the face – winging out from the eyes. This is the simplest and most effective 'face-lifting' trick there is. For the lips, an eye pencil can double as a lip liner. Outline the lips first, then fill in with lipstick, avoiding pale pinks and true orange colours.

LEFT: *Without make-up.* ABOVE: *After applying the minimum make-up for maximum effect. In the morning, carefully apply foundation and loose powder, then eye make-up. Here a grey eye pencil, grey shadow over the eye lid, darker blue-grey on outer part of lid and cream highlighter on brow. Mascara and lipstick complete the effect. Take with you pressed powder, blusher and lipstick for touching up.*

Choosing and using foundation

A good foundation evens up your skin tone and helps to hide any trouble spots. Beige or cream tones help to tone down a florid skin. Pink tones emphasise a fair skin and add glowing colour to a sallow skin. Neutral beige tones give a delicate look and tone down a ruddy complexion. Beige tones are generally more flattering to older skins. Golden honey tones promote a healthy, outdoor glow. It is a mistake to try to alter your colouring too much with foundation – choose a colour within two shades lighter or darker than your skin tone.

Foundations are available in creams, cakes, gels and liquids. The texture of a foundation can help you achieve your ideal skin tone. A liquid foundation is ideal; it provides a light protective film with a fairly good coverage. The secret is to dot the liquid all over your face and neck and smooth in lightly with downward strokes. Blend quickly and carefully, especially around the hairline and jaw, making sure that the colour fades out with no obvious demarcation lines.

To find the shade that's best for you, compare the colour in the bottle or tube with the skin tone on the inside of your wrist or on your neck in daylight.

Using powder

Over half of the most common problems with make-up are caused by not wearing powder. This is invariably the reason why make-up disappears by 11 o'clock in the morning and why it becomes greasy-looking very quickly after application. Powder takes the shine off your face and gives skin a velvety finish as well. The best kind to use is translucent; colour should come from your foundation, not your powder. It is also easier to achieve the 'see through' look if you use a loose powder rather than a pressed one.

RIGHT: *Applying foundation. Dot on sparingly over your forehead, cheeks, nose and chin, then smooth in gently from hairline to jawline. Use your fingertips or a barely damp sponge to obtain a thin even film. Apply foundation over moisturiser and under powder for a lovely, lasting effect.*

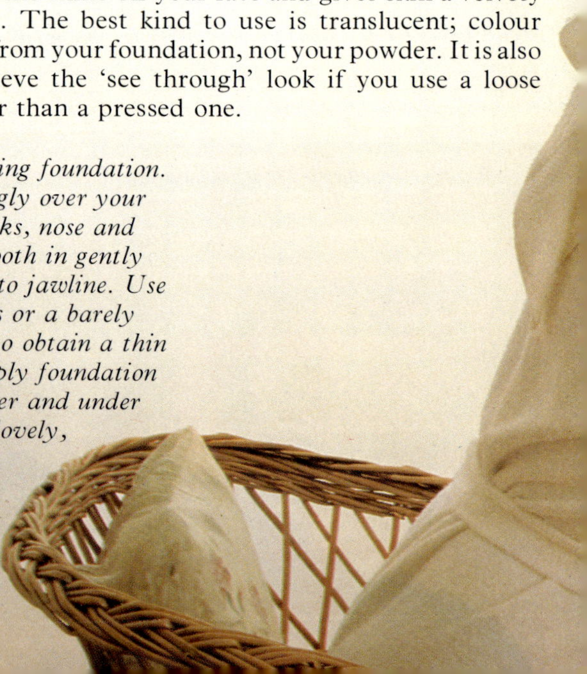

To apply powder: In the mornings, pat loose powder on lightly with cotton wool or a powder puff over your foundation, then dust off the excess. Artists' brushes, the plump fluffy sable ones, are also ideal for applying powder. For the smoothest finish, always blend in powder using downward movements. This is the direction in which facial hair and down grow. If you stroke your face in the opposite direction, you will fluff up the fine hair and make it more visible.
To finish: After applying foundation and powder, for good measure, wring out a cotton wool ball in icy cold water and lightly pat it all over your face. This 'sets' the make-up and helps its 'staying power'.

Choosing and using face colour

Face blushers are a whole new category of colouring products which have evolved from rouge. To use blushers properly you must appreciate the principles of light and shade, then apply them to your face shape. The blusher family is made up of three different groups.

There are the natural looking peach and pinky tones which add colour to the cheek area. Shaders are the darker tawny, brick, rust and plum tones which literally help shade away specific areas. Highlighters, which are usually creamy luminous tones, do just the reverse and draw attention to certain areas. Difficulties usually arise when it is not appreciated that all three varieties shouldn't just be plonked on the cheeks. The pinks and peaches are right for the cheeks; they should be applied high on the cheekbone. Shader is more likely to go under the cheeks to create pretty 'hollows'. Highlighter is applied very high on the cheekbones – above the natural-looking shade.

Brush-on colour is applied after powder. Cream or liquid goes on before powder; use the dot and blend technique, rather as if you are applying foundation. Not sure where your cheekbones are? Find them with your fingertips. Then apply pink or peach 'cheek' colour lightly along the bone, blending

CORRECTING FACE SHAPES WITH BLUSHER

LEFT: *Round face. Apply 'natural' cheek colour along the cheekbone; shader to help minimise fullness around the chin.*

RIGHT: *Long face. Apply 'natural' cheek colour along, and highlighter above, the cheekbone; shade out the end of the nose and the chin.*

up and out towards your hairline. Don't blush too close to your nose or lower than the tip of it or you lose that 'lift.'

When you are feeling really tired, there are other 'face-lifting' tricks to try. Brush on colour lightly along the top of the forehead, under the chin and over the bridge of the nose. When it's your eyes that are looking weary, wing colour out to the temples and in again, just above the eyebrows.

Where to put shader and highlighter really depends on your face shape. If you're not sure what yours is, get another opinion and go on to master the technique of light and shade. For instance, a round face can take a dusting of shader to help minimise fullness in the chin, and doesn't usually need highlighter. A long face can take lots of highlighter, well back above the cheekbones to give an illusion of fullness and width. If your nose and chin are on the long side too, a little shader applied to the end of each can make them appear shorter. A square face can take shader well down towards the jaw and highlighter fluffed really high on the cheekbones, to widen the upper part of the face. A triangular-shaped face can take a lot of highlighter both sides of the forehead and a dusting of shader from the ear lobes, fading out at the chin.

Whatever the shape of your face, check that you haven't created an unnatural effect by applying too much blusher.

LEFT: *Square face. Apply 'natural' cheek colour along, and highlight above the cheekbone and shade down towards the jaw.*

RIGHT: *Triangular face. Apply 'natural' cheek colour along the cheekbone, shader on the sides of the face, highlighter on the edges of your forehead.*

Choosing and using eye make-up

Aim to build up a wardrobe of eye colours and wear two or three at a time in different combinations. One suggestion is the blue/primrose eye (see right); you will find more colour schemes on pages 46 and 47. The secret of blending two or three colours successfully is to let them overlap to avoid hard edges. Powder shadows are easily applied and blended; so are creams – but be sure to blend the crease-resistant variety quickly because they dry soon after application. If you are over 35, choose matt textures rather than irridescent ones for the actual eyelid; wear irridescence as a highlighter under the brow bone. Powder shadows stay in place better when applied to lids which have been slightly moisturised.

If you have less-than-perfect eyes you need to use neutral contouring shades; the correct shades used in the right places before you apply your actual eye colour scheme can make problems disappear. To identify your eye type, see Correcting eye shapes (pages 44–5).

Apart from eye shadow, you will probably want to apply pencil liner and mascara. A soft eye pencil makes the eyes seem larger and the lashes thicker. Draw a thin line along the base of the upper lashes, then outline the lower lashes from the centre of the lid outwards. If you don't like the idea of a continuous line, use pencil to dot on colour between the lashes and you will still achieve the lash-thickening effect. Blend the line, if you like, with your fingertip or blur the edge with a fine brush.

Another reason for wearing eyeliner is to give your eyes a more expressive shape. When this is your intention, start the line at the inner corner of the eye and widen it a bit towards the centre, thinning out again at the outer corner. It's a good rule to match the colour of your eye pencil to that of your eye shadow or mascara.

When you stroke on mascara, be sure to coat lashes all the way to the tips. For a lavish look, coat the tops first, then brush up from underneath to curve lashes slightly. When the mascara has dried, separate the lashes with a clean dry brush or wand. As a colour guide: brunettes should wear black mascara; blondes and fair redheads, brown or charcoal; everyone else should use dark brown.

You may need to shape and colour your brows with eyebrow pencil. If the colour is right, you can also use the pencil for outlining eyes and lips. Never draw on one hard line and don't colour the actual skin if there is a hair you can pull into line instead. For the best light-handed approach, curve the heel of your hand around the cheekbone and draw in the shape with light flicks from the wrist.

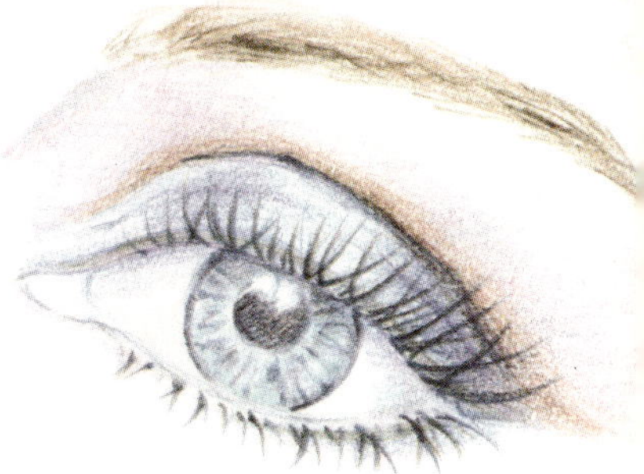

THE BLUE/PRIMROSE EYE
BELOW: *Outline lids with blue-grey pencil and blend darker blue shadow over and beyond the pencil line.*

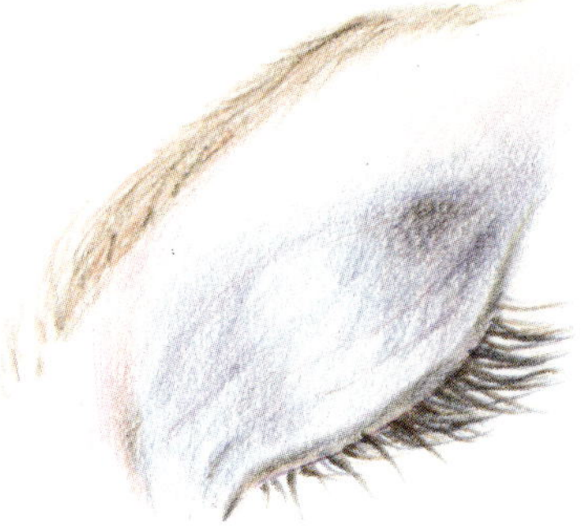

ABOVE: *Use brown pencil on eyelid crease and outer corner.* TOP: *Dust pale lemon shadow all over eye. Then apply mascara and touch up with blue-grey pencil.*

LEFT: *High-set brows.*

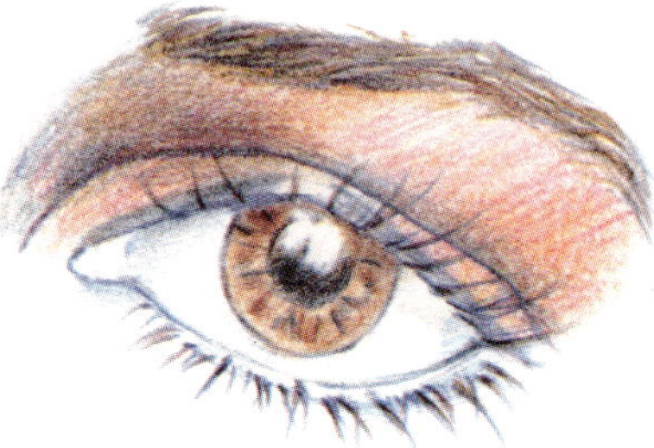

RIGHT: *Deep-set eyes.*

LEFT: *Narrow almond eyes.*

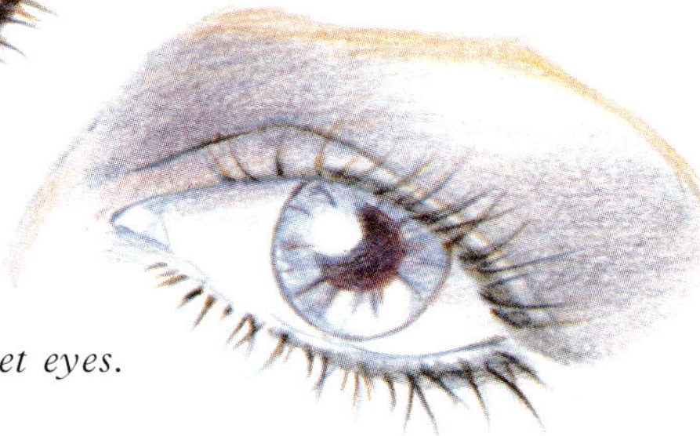

RIGHT: *Wide-set eyes.*

Correcting eye shapes

By using light and dark neutral eye shadows and pencil, it is possible to correct any eye shape problem. You must do this after putting on foundation and before going on to apply your actual eye colour scheme.

High-set brows: To underplay the lid area and minimise the space between brows and eyes, apply a pale shadow, such as mauve, from lashes to brows, then use a grey pencil to outline the eyes.

Deep-set eyes: A 'wash' of brick-coloured shadow from lashes to brows 'reduces' the eyebrow bones. An irridescent pearl grey pencil emphasises lashes, which helps bring the eyes forward.

Narrow almond eyes: A gold colour, blended from lashes to brows, highlights eyes. A grey line along the eyelid crease is also needed. Use a black pencil to outline lower lashes and create an illusion of depth.

LEFT: *Small close-set eyes.*

RIGHT: *Small wide-set eyes.*

LEFT: *Prominent eyelids.*

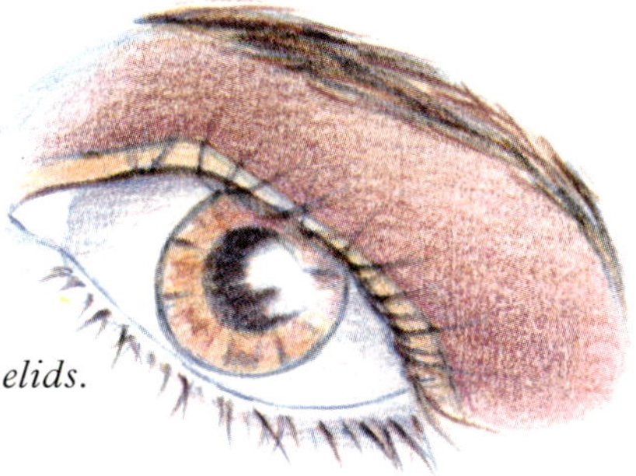

RIGHT: *Hidden eyelids.*

Wide-set eyes: A frosted grey shadow, on the lids and smoothed high into the corners, helps draw eyes closer together. A darker grey pencil used to partially outline the lids helps to define the eyes; outline top and bottom lids, working from the outer corner and fading out as you reach the centre.
Small close-set eyes: Light brown shadow from lashes to brows 'widens' the lids. Use a dark liner just at the inner and outer corners.
Small wide-set eyes: Moss green smoothed on the lids and high into the corners brings eyes together. A black outline around the outer corners helps to define and enlarge the eyes.
Prominent eyelids: To make the lids seem to recede, apply a wash of brown shadow, from lashes to crease line; play up the area above with beige highlighter. Use brown eye liner.
Hidden eyelids: Reverse the technique for prominent lids: apply beige shadow to the eyelid area, and brown shadow above – up to brows. Draw the thinnest eye line possible.

Eye catching colours

Almost any colour scheme goes as long as the colours are subtly applied and blended.

For dark eyes: One of the most effective colour schemes is the mauve/brown eye (see above). Apply deep mauve shadow all over the lid, with beige-brown as a highlighter under the brow. Outline the eye with a grey-brown shade.

Also for dark eyes, consider a combination of pink/blue. Apply rose shadow on the lid, grey-blue shadow to emphasise the outer half of the lid, and dark grey as a liner.

There is also the grey/copper scheme for dark eyes. Apply silvery-grey shadow all over the lid, a touch of copper shadow in the centre of the lid, and use dark grey to outline.

For grey eyes: Try a mixture of brick/plum colours. Apply the brick tone all over the lid and use the plum shadow to emphasise centre of lid. Use a tawny brown pencil to outline.

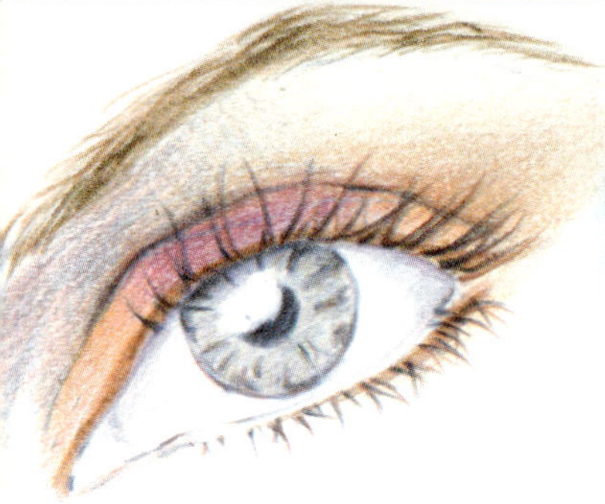

ABOVE: *For grey eyes, try a mixture of brick/plum.*
ABOVE RIGHT: *For hazel eyes, try a brick/ turquoise scheme.*
RIGHT: *For blue eyes, silver/plum is effective.*
OPPOSITE PAGE: *For dark eyes, there's mauve/brown.*

A brick/green colour scheme also works well for grey eyes. Apply pale brick shadow to the whole eye area, then use a dark green shadow on the lid and a dark green pencil to outline.

For really dark grey eyes, there is the mauve/pink eye. Use mauve shadow on the lid, pale pink as a highlighter under the brow and dark grey, or even black, to outline.

For blue eyes: A silver/plum colour combination is really effective. Apply plum shadow over the lid, then dust over with silver. Use silver-grey to outline – the darker the better.

Also for blue eyes is the grey/brick combination. Shade the whole lid with brick and cover with grey. To outline, use grey.

For a true blue scheme, apply pale blue over the whole eye area. Use darker blue on the outer half of the lid and a similar shade for outlining the eye. Put a touch of cream highlighter shadow into the extreme inner corner of the lid.

For hazel eyes: There is the brick/turquoise combination, Use pale brick shadow on the inner half of the lid, turquoise on the outer half. Use tawny brown to outline.

Beige/grey gives a lovely sophisticated subtlety to hazel eyes. Apply grey-gold shadow all over the eye area, then grey shadow to the lid. Use green to outline.

Primrose/green is pretty. Dust primrose shadow on inner half of lid, moss green on outer half. Use dark green to outline.

For green eyes: There is the brick/gold scheme. Apply pale goldshadow over the whole eye area, then dust brick over the lid only; use tawny amber to outline.

Choosing and using lipsticks

Eye make-up and lipstick go together. Wear one without the other and your face will look out of balance. A brush or a lip liner pencil is almost essential, if you want to emphasise the shape of your mouth. And it's a good idea to outline with a strong colour, deep pink, plum or brick, then fill in with a paler frosted shade. This technique gives a lovely luminous effect. (See opposite: a tawny brick outlines lips, a pale brick is used to colour them in.) As a general rule, blot frosted lipsticks, but not matt ones. And, for touching up during the day, carry lip gloss with you; it is a mistake to keep piling on more and more lipstick.

Unless you are really expert with make-up, it's not a good idea to start tampering with the shape of your lips by blotting out with foundation and drawing in new outlines. The clever approach is to use colour to create the illusion of a different shape. This method is less time-consuming and likely to be much more successful.

Full lips: To condense this shape, choose a clear, bright colour. Always apply lip gloss before you stroke on the colour. Lipstick applied over a gloss doesn't appear as dark and has a sheerer texture.

Ill-matched lips: Often lips don't match each other in size. The top lip is thinner and smaller than the bottom. One lip colour over-all just exaggerates this, so it is a good idea to use two different shades, both in the same colour spectrum, but one slightly deeper than the other. Use the deeper shade on the top lip.

Thin lips: Warm amber to brick tones are best for this lip shape. Outline thin lips with a deep tone, then fill in with a paler frosted shade.

CORRECTING LIP SHAPES

ABOVE: *Full lips.*

ABOVE: *Ill-matched lips.*

ABOVE: *Thin lips.*

ABOVE: *For a perfect lipline, start by steadying your hand. Prop your elbow on the dressing table or let your chin support your little finger. Relax your mouth.*

Whether you're using a pencil or a lipbrush, carefully outline the bow first, then draw in the corners and connect with a straight line. Gradually build up the lower lip curve. Then fill in with lipstick or again, if you prefer, a brush.

Correcting face faults

By using colour carefully, you can do a great deal towards correcting any facial irregularities. Your palette is the whole beige to brown spectrum, taking in everything from very pale to quite dark shades and including all sorts of consistencies: tinted moisturiser, foundation, powder, sticks of concealer make-up, specialist camouflage preparations, face blushers, shaders and highlighters, and eye shadows.

The golden rule is this: any part of your face you want to make smaller make darker; anything you want to emphasise, make lighter.

For bags under the eyes: Use a foundation one shade darker than the foundation you are using all over your face and brush it precisely on the bag, in a thin line; it should be crescent-shaped.

For dark rings under the eyes: Use a pale make-up concealer stick or foundation one shade paler than the one you are applying elsewhere. Alternatively, a white or cream eye shadow highlighter, which is too pale to be worn on its own here, is effective when applied under foundation.

For noses of all shapes and sizes: Slim a nose by putting dark foundation down the sides, blending well at the edges. Make a nose look straighter by applying a light line down the centre; use foundation or pale concealer stick and blend well. Shorten a nose by putting dark foundation right under the tip and blending in well.

For nose to mouth lines: Use a light make-up concealer stick. Transfer the product onto a brush and trace a fine line along the groove; this is the same technique as the one used for bags under the eyes.

For a mouth that sags at the corners: Use a brush to apply a touch of light concealer stick to the area.

For freckles: The right foundation is helpful if you want to hide freckles. Choose a shade that's a little darker than your skin tone and a little lighter than your freckles. Follow it with pressed powder in the shade closest to your skin tone. If you have some particularly giant freckles you can cover them up with an opaque make-up. Freckles are intensified by the pigmentation which comes from the sun and certain climatic conditions. In summer, when you are probably leaving off make-up anyway, you might prefer to even out the freckle areas – especially on the cheeks – by fluffing on a tawny face shader which merges well with freckle patterns.

For more serious skin blemishes and scars: Use special masking and toning creams which help camouflage. These are of a more dense texture and are more heavily pigmented than ordinary make-up. If they are applied carefully, in the right

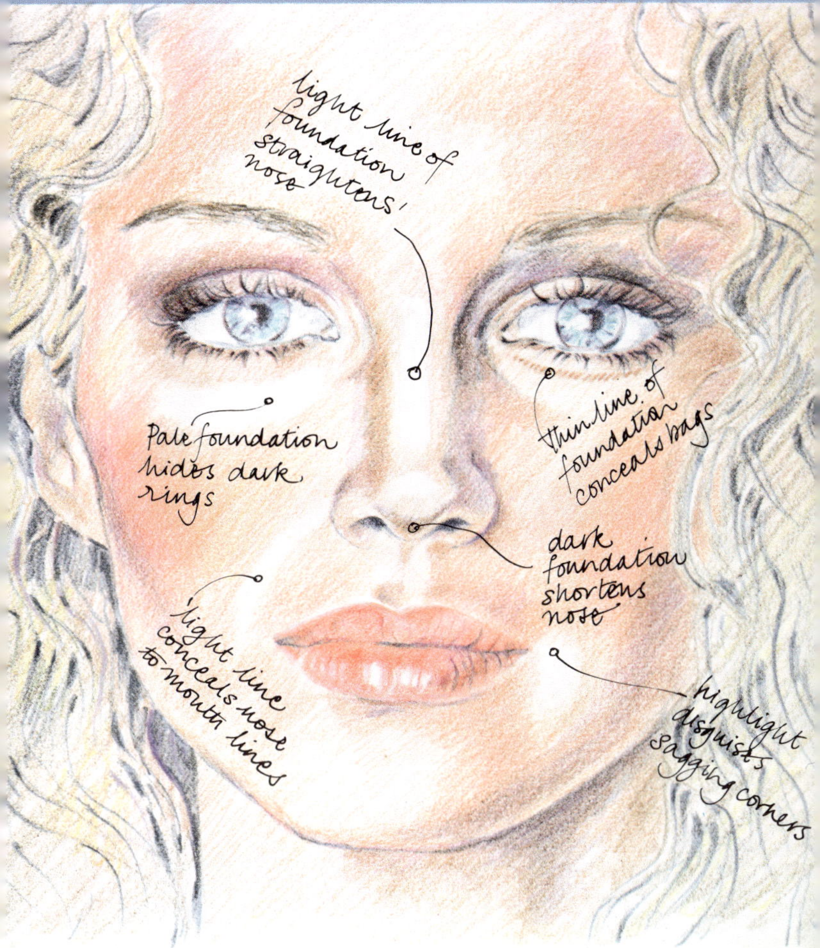

combination of shades, these cosmetics are practically indistinguishable on the skin.

For high colouring: Apply a beige-toned foundation then set with loose powder; this should provide sufficient camouflage. High colouring is usually concentrated on the cheeks and around the nostrils. It stems from tiny cracks just beneath the surface of the skin into which traces of blood can escape. Fine sensitive skins are particularly prone to these thread veins. If the condition is quite serious and foundation and powder doesn't provide effective cover, consider a tinted moisturiser with a slight green cast to counteract the floridity; you can then go on to apply foundation and powder as usual.

For moles: Make up your mind whether you are going to tone down the odd mole with special masking make-up or make the most of it as a beauty spot.

Special considerations for the over-fifties

Over a certain age you don't make-up you 'make down', which simply means that the older the skin, the more fragile it becomes and the less make-up it needs. This doesn't impose any restrictions on the number of items used, but it does mean that it is more important than ever before to apply them lightly and subtly for maximum effect and minimum coverage. Remember when you apply make-up that the 'canvas' is wearing thin.

Learn to warm your foundation in the palm of your hand; cold application drags the skin. And fight the temptation to put on too much foundation, especially around the eye area; the skin here almost inevitably darkens in colour with age. The secret is to have two shades of foundation; one to go all over, a lighter one for the area under the eyes.

Most women give up powder after a certain age, but it is not necessary to do so. Powder is still the best way to set make-up for the day. Get the better of wrinkles by gripping the powder puff or a pad of cotton wool between forefinger and thumb, then hold the skin taut and press powder down onto the skin with a light 'heeling' movement. Always dust off any excess; it's important to avoid a powdered look – that's very ageing.

There's a lot you can do to 'lift' your face with colour. Eyes tend to narrow as they get older, so use a pale eye-shadow colour – preferably not blue. Use this as a wash over the whole eye area, blending up and outwards towards the temples; remember that lines that go up look younger than lines that droop. Green eye shadow is a good choice; it suits most skin and eye colourings. Use a pale green for the lids, then edge along the lashes with a darker green, blurring the application with the fingertip. For staying power on the lids, mix powder

LEFT: *Without make-up.* RIGHT: *After applying the minimum of make-up for maximum effect. Foundation and powder together are essential. Delicate toning shadows are ideal for eyes. In this case green; pale green as background and a darker moss shade to emphasize the base of the lashes. One light coat of mascara is flattering, too. Make sure that your blusher and lipstick tone for the best effect.*

shadow with a little moisturiser and apply carefully.

Be very careful with mascara – apply one coat only. Powder lashes first if you want to make them look thicker. Avoid using black; there are lovely greys and browns which will suit you better.

A touch of blusher makes the face look younger. For the right place to put it, feel with your fingers where your cheekbone starts below the temple. Blend in the colour along the bone, pushing up slightly against it. Don't apply blusher above your cheekbones or too near your nose and avoid a downward line; finish with a flick upwards.

One of the best ways to arrive at the right consistency and colour of blusher is to mix a little of your lipstick colour choice with moisturiser or cold cream. To team with green eye make-up, warm rust is ideal.

Special effects for the bride and mother

For most brides, making up to wearing white means a completely new approach to beauty. The effect of an all-white or cream wedding dress and veil is to create an aura which seems to suffuse the face and transform complexion colour. Girls who are not in the habit of wearing anything pale or pastel-toned might well find that their usual make-up needs playing up or playing down. This also applies to the bridesmaids or the bride's mum – if she's wearing something paler than she would normally choose.

The first essential for the leading ladies in the wedding group is a flattering shade of foundation. If your dress is dazzling white and the bridesmaids' or mother's choice green, blue or lemon, choose a foundation one shade warmer than the one you usually wear. If your dress is a warm cream, with pink or gold for bridesmaids or mum, consider foundations one shade paler than usual.

Skin texture should present no problems, if you plan wedding day looks far in advance and eat sensibly for a slim figure, shining hair, glossy nails and a clear skin. Just in case excitement produces an isolated spot on the actual day, match a medicated camouflage stick to your foundation colour. To encourage your make-up to last all day, apply translucent loose powder over your foundation. And carry with you a compact of translucent pressed powder for touching up your make-up occasionally throughout the day with no build-up of colour.

Blusher is the most important part of wedding day make-up. Choose rose-pink or subdued amber shades to emphasise the cheekbones and forget about reds and plums – these come out far too dark in photographs. A pale and pretty irridescent blusher always looks good fluffed on to the brow and winging out from the cheekbones – to emphasise the eyes; this gives a shimmering effect to the make-up and 'rebuffs' any shadows cast by the veil.

For photographs, the paler the eye-shadow, the more noticeable your eyes. This doesn't mean that you are restricted to green or blue. Try pale amber, warm beige or cool lavender. Choose grey liner and mascara if you are brunette, brown colours if you are blonde. Ideally, wear one pale shadow all over the lid; use brown or grey in the crease line and to outline the upper and lower lids. Don't over-do the mascara.

For lips, choose a medium tone lipstick in the same colour spectrum as your blusher. And either mix the lipstick with lip gloss or apply gloss on top of your lip colour, for a beautiful luminous effect.

ABOVE: *The bride wears a paler foundation than usual and translucent loose powder; a matching compact is to hand. She needs two blushers – one for cheeks and a paler version to fluff on forehead and tops of cheeks. Eye make-up consists of shadow, pencil to emphasize crease line and lashes, and mascara. Lipstick is topped with gloss.*

The bride's mum is wearing a cream blouse, so the same rule applies for a cool foundation and translucent powder. Because her coat and hat are blue, she needs a more vibrant pink blusher and a blue-pink lipstick tone. Her eye make-up is grey-blue.

PARTY EYES IN CLOSE-UP
LEFT: *For a brunette – sparkling blue shadow on lid, pearly highlighter on brow-bone; brown along crease.*
RIGHT: *For a blonde – there's glittery pink on the lids and creamy highlighter up to the brow-bone.*

Special effects for a party

Choose colours that glow: Candle light or any subdued lighting is very flattering but gives little light. To be seen at your best avoid dark foundations or muted tones; your skin tone should be clear and light-reflectant, so that your face glows. Choose clear colours for eyes, lips and cheeks; muddy in-between shades just don't look as good in night light as they do during the day.

Try textures that gleam: Several kinds of make-up now come with glitter added, as well as in their regular form. There are foundations with a touch of shimmer, frosted lipsticks and lip glosses, and irridescent face powders, eye shadows, cheek blushers, shaders and highlighters. And, with the possible exception of lipstick, any one of these items can double up in all sorts of ways – highlighting temples, the crest of the cheekbones, the shoulders even. The purpose of all these products is to light up your face, but they can also make you look frostbitten or garish if applied with too heavy a hand. Girls still in their teens can get away with wearing everything in the glitter spectrum at once. Over-twenties need to wear it more subtly by combining carefully chosen glitter with their normal make-up to create a lovely glamorous effect. Here are two foolproof ways of applying glitter effectively.

Party effects for brunettes: The colour scheme illustrated above (left) is particularly good. To achieve this look, apply your usual foundation and powder, then dust on a frosted cheek blusher. Use one or two of the lightly frosted brush-on eye shadows and slick a frosty gloss over your lipstick. Choose vibrant pink for both lipstick and cheek colour. Sparkling blue is the shade for the eyelids, with brown accentuating the eyelid crease and winging right round the outer corner of the eye. Shimmering cream highlighter plays up the eyebrow bone.

Remember it's important to choose clear colours for lips, eyes and cheeks; as long as all these areas are equally bright, the results look good. It's only when the balance of colour is wrong that the whole effect can look overdone.

Party effects for blondes: Here's how to achieve the stunningly attractive scheme illustrated above (right). Apply make-up just as you usually do. Then fluff translucent powder, in a gold-fleck, silver or opalescent shade, all over your face (except your nose – shimmer here looks too much like shine). Pink is the colour to use for eyes, cheeks and lips. Keeping to one colour tone, like this, is the way to achieve a really luminous make-up. Pink is good with a blue or black outfit; gingery tones are best for a green or yellow outfit.

Hair Care

Nature determines the texture, natural bend and growth rate of your hair. The rest is up to you and depends largely on how – and how often – you use hairbrush, shampoo, conditioning cream and other aids to gloriously healthy hair.

Of course, all sorts of conditions can affect hair health and, as always, prevention is easier than cure. Generally, if you eat to keep your skin healthy, you will find your hair is healthy too. From then on, correct care will help maintain the hair and scalp in a healthy state.

Brushing
Aim to brush your hair every day. Brushing stimulates the flow of blood to the scalp, removes dirt and debris from the hair and helps spread sebum, which is produced at the base of the hair, along the hair shaft. Brushing smooths down the scales of the cuticle, the outer layer of each hair, and gives a glossy sheen. It also helps to subdue 'static'. All hair types benefit from brushing.
Choosing your hairbrush: The correct brush shape for your hair will depend on its texture; i.e. fine, average or coarse. The right bristle consistency will depend upon whether your hair is thick, average or thin. For coarse hair, use a semi-radial shape – one with a 'half-moon' of bristles. For average hair, try a complete radial brush – one with bristles all round. If you have fine hair, choose a paddle (flat) shape or a radial brush. For thick hair, a mixture of nylon and bristle is best. An all-bristle brush is good for thin hair.
How to brush: Always brush (or comb, for that matter) from the roots of the hair to the ends. And always brush your hair dry – never wet. Brushing wet hair can cause cuticle damage which results in split ends. Brush before shampooing to distribute the natural oils right through the hair.

If you have long hair, use two brushes rather than one. Put your head down and brush from the nape down towards the ends of the hair, to coax much more volume into your hair. As you brush, you will find that the bristles penetrate more and more easily until you are touching the scalp each time with the bristles. Don't hack at your hair and don't flatten it down to your head; lift it in wide curves. Brush as rapidly as you like but don't flick the brushes harshly when you reach the ends of your hair. Finally, bring your head up again and brush down from the top of your scalp.

Shampooing

Shampooing the hair cleanses it and makes it springy and fragrant. Choose your shampoo according to the condition of your scalp.

A dry scalp feels 'tight' and can become so tense that headaches result. Over-shampooing can remove all trace of natural oil. Try diluting shampoo with water before applying it to hair.

With a greasy scalp, the skin is quite pliable – you can move your scalp under your hand. For this scalp type, use warm, not hot, water and give an extra final rinse.

A normal scalp looks healthy and has a good, normal skin colour. If your scalp is normal, concentrate on it more than your hair with the first application of shampoo. With the second, massage suds into the bulk of the hair.

With a dandruff-prone scalp which visibly sheds scales, make sure you rinse off every speck of shampoo and wash combs and brushes at the same time.

How often should you shampoo? As often as is necessary for your kind of scalp – once a week certainly, but perhaps as frequently as every day. As long as you are using the right shampoo, you needn't worry, either about drying out your scalp, or encouraging a greasy scalp to become more oily.

The shampoo drill: 1. First brush out all tangles; brushing also removes loose dirt and dandruff. **2.** Massage your entire scalp, briskly but gently, with a rotating movement of hands and fingertips. **3.** Wet your hair all over with warm water and either spot shampoo all over the whole scalp, or pour shampoo into the palm of your hand and apply it to the hair. **4.** Lather well and massage the shampoo well into your scalp with the same massage movement – a rotation of hands and fingertips (not nails). On this first application, concentrate mostly on shampooing the scalp rather than the hair; your scalp needs laundering most. **5.** Rinse off with warm water. **6.** Lather again and repeat massaging movement, paying special attention to the area around the hairline where make-up and debris can collect. Then rub the ends of your hair between your palms carefully with suds. *Note*: If you are washing your hair almost every day this second application of shampoo is not usually necessary. Equally, if your scalp is very greasy you might prefer to stick at one shampoo; over-enthusiastic shampooing can stimulate the sebaceous glands to produce more oil. **7.** Rinse the entire head thoroughly. Rinse and rinse again until you are absolutely certain all soap is rinsed away. A shower attachment giving a constant flow of water is ideal for this; you can just continue rinsing until the water runs clear. Any shampoo not rinsed away will have a dulling effect on your hair. **8.** Finish with a cold water rinse to give your hair more shine and gloss, then squeeze gently to remove excess water. At this stage, you may want to apply conditioner (see page 64). **9.** Blot your hair with a towel. Never rub too fiercely; apart from the danger of damaging the hair, you can also stir up the sebaceous glands to renewed activity – something to avoid, if your scalp is inclined to be greasy. **10.** Go on to dry your hair immediately, or wrap it in a towel, turban-style for a few minutes. The towel will absorb all the moisture and when you unwind it, your hair will be at the damp-dry stage.

BELOW: *Massaging the shampoo well into the scalp with the fingertips, using a brisk rotating movement of the hands (step 4, the shampoo drill).*

Massage

Massage is marvellous for easing a tight dry scalp. It also activates the tiny oil glands at the base of each hair, encouraging them to lubricate each hair shaft just enough for elasticity and 'bounce'.

Dry-massage: Work over your scalp in three easy stages. 1. Start at the nape of the neck and work towards the crown. Use your thumbs only to begin with and pay particular attention to the whole neck area because that's where tension is most likely to build up; you should be able to feel any little knots of tension. Leave your thumbs in position at the nape of the neck until you have reached the crown with your fingertips; work in circular movements and use the pads of the fingers – never dig in with the nails. 2. Now work from the temples up to the crown, placing hands either side of your head, with thumbs braced to support the fingers. Manipulate the scalp with the pads of the fingers, as before. 3. Now concentrate on the area around the hairline which really benefits from massage because the skin here is very fine and the supply of natural nourishment less good. Equally, this is the area where make-up and debris collect; massage helps to get rid of any build-up.

Wet-massage: This method is performed with hair conditioner, prior to shampooing. It helps stimulate hair growth – especially when the hair has been badly damaged through over-exposure to the elements. To wet-massage, start at the nape of the neck with the fingers spread out, and travel slowly towards the crown, moving the scalp with kneading movements. Repeat from the temples and forehead.

OPPOSITE: *Dry Massage. Work from the nape of the neck up to the crown.* BELOW: *Then massage from the temples to the crown.*

BELOW: *Finally concentrate on the fine skin around the hairline, which particularly benefits from massage, as it receives little nourishment.*

ABOVE: *Combing conditioner gently through hair to ensure even distribution (step 2, conditioning routine).*

Conditioning

Choose conditioner for the state of your hair – which isn't the same as the state of your scalp. The most normal hair conditions are as follows. 1. Dry unmanageable hair usually has a fuzzy outline and often goes with dry scalp and coarse hair. 2. Lank, dull hair frequently goes with a greasy or dandruff-prone scalp and average to coarse hair. 3. Splitting, or brittle ends often go with a normal scalp and occur in all hair-texture types.

For dry dull or brittle hair, conditioner is a must. It coats the hair and makes it smooth and shiny. Conditioned hair no longer feels rough and it has extra fullness and body. Lank dull hair needs conditioning too – to give it body. There are totally oil-free conditioners which are ideal for this hair type. Even if your hair is normal, make a concentrated effort to massage conditioner onto the hair ends; by doing so you can often help prevent injury to the hair shaft with the inevitable outcome – split ends. When these occur, the ends of the hair literally open up like a 'Y' and a split can travel right up the hair, leaving a series of broken wisps all over the head.

Remember conditioner is the invisible 'raincoat' which will help any hair type stand up to bad weather. Curly hair swells up and becomes difficult to handle in damp weather; conditioner helps curb this tendency. Long fine hair goes limp at the first sign of dampness; conditioner adds body. Fine wavy hair goes wispy; conditioner helps keep it smooth.

Conditioner is normally applied after shampooing. It will close any open cuticle scales and replace the natural oils which protect the hair. Left on the hair for a minute or two, a conditioner acts as a detangler and adds shine, body and lustre to the hair. Apply conditioner once the hair has been thoroughly rinsed after shampooing. Never massage conditioner into the scalp. Usually, you will only need to apply conditioner from the middle to the ends of the hair; the roots don't normally need it unless the hair is bleached.

The conditioning routine: **1.** Pour conditioner into the palm of the hand, then gently squeeze onto the hair. **2.** Comb the conditioner through the hair to ensure an even spread. If the comb doesn't slide through easily, don't tug at the hair. Rather hold the jet of water from the spray head behind the comb and let the force of the water mix with the conditioner and smooth the path for the comb. **3.** Leave conditioner on for a minute or two before rinsing hair thoroughly with warm water. **4.** If your hair is very dry, reapply conditioner to the ends, about the last 5 cm (2 inches), and then rinse lightly. **5.** Blot dry with a towel or wrap the hair in a towel-turban which will absorb excess moisture. Never rub at the hair with a towel after conditioning or you will undo all the good work of the conditioner.

Deep-conditioning formulae: These are for use regularly once a month, or every six weeks, or for times when the hair has become badly damaged through over-exposure to wind or sunshine, sea water or chlorinated water. For this routine: **1.** Massage your scalp, working up warmth. **2.** Part the hair four ways and smooth conditioner onto each part, starting at the roots if the hair there is showing signs of damage; otherwise begin half-way down the hair shaft. **3.** Wrap your hair in a towel turban and leave your hair for at least 20 minutes. **4.** Shampoo your hair in the usual way.

Choosing your style
Thinking of changing your hairstyle? Then don't ask more of your hair than it can possibly give. For instance, thin limp hair will never look good in an elaborate arrangement; coarse curly hair cannot be persuaded to give a smooth bob effect. Apart from the texture of your hair, other considerations are the shape of your face, your features and general proportions. Healthiest hair is always shortish hair because it never gets long enough and old enough to be damaged. Long hair can be healthy if it's looked after well and trimmed regularly.

One length hair, blunt cut: See above. The important thing to remember with this style is that hair never grows evenly all over the scalp – so you can't keep a clean shape-holding edge unless it's scissor-cut regularly. Every six weeks to two months is just about right. Don't persevere with this style if your hair is very fine and gets greasy quickly or if it tends to split.

If you are into your thirties and still clinging to the shoulder-length style of your teens, maybe it's time to think again. Wear your hair like this if it's in good condition, and you have a good forehead and hairline; if necessary you can camouflage an uneven hairline by selecting tiny wisps and trimming them short.

LEFT: *One length, blunt cut for medium to long hair. A band keeps hair off the face.*

ABOVE: *A slightly graduated bob cut; the hair brushed off the face at the sides.*

This length of hair can also be plaited or braided, or worn up in a French pleat or a top knot. Braid it before going to bed and you will have a gently rippled effect when you comb out the next morning. For quicker 'sets', you can brush and blow dry or use pin curls. But with this amount of hair you must pin curl the hair damp and not remove the pins until the hair is completely dry; otherwise the weight of the damp hair will make all the curl drop out.

A bob shape, slightly graduated: See above. This is a very versatile style and absolutely right for anyone growing out a fringe. Brush the hair slightly away from the face at the sides and it's good for all face shapes, except those that are long. Brush it back and away from the face at the sides and it has a really slimming effect on a round or heavy face.

After shampooing, to coax maximum volume into this style, brush and blow dry the hair with the head down. Then, when your hair is completely dry, throw your head back and double brush for maximum shine and manageability. This step is particularly important if your hair is fine.

Short, layered hair: See above. This style is ideal for anyone with fine hair and plenty of it. Naturally curly hair is also very suitable. You can brush and blow dry it for a flat, sleek effect, or make it extra curly with rollers or curling tongs, then finger dry it – just to trace the pattern of the natural movement in the hair. This style flatters heart-shaped and oval faces but isn't so good for a round face. It can work for a square face, if the hair is combed in the right direction; i.e. into soft rounded lines, waving over the brow and with enough fullness on top to detract from the width of the forehead and chin. The style is also good for a long face, providing you keep the sides full and the ends flicked up.

Hair as short as this needs to be trimmed regularly; every four to five weeks is ideal. And in just one trim or cut, short hair lends itself to a complete change of style. Clever scissoring means hair can be persuaded to fall forwards instead of backwards, or swept to one side or the other. Short hair really is versatile – in a way that long hair never can be.

A word of warning: if you are undecided about having your hair cut short or very short, before you do anything, take a sharp look at yourself in a full-length mirror and ask yourself this question. Are you planning to perch a gamin haircut on a large frame? Remember for the best overall effect your hairdo

LEFT: *A short layered cut, made extra curly by styling with curling tongs.*

RIGHT: *Medium length, layered hairstyle, ideal for fine hair.*

should be in proportion to the rest of you. Similarly, a mass of wavy long hair can overpower a petite figure. Make up your mind before you are sitting in the hairdresser's chair. Always give a new style long and careful thought before you book an appointment for a drastic change.

Medium-length hair, very layered: See above. This style is marvellous for fine hair; layering it like this gives it much more interest. The fringe is also very layered to give a flattering effect. This style combines the advantages of short and long hair, without being too conservative.

Layered hair suits most people because it's very good for softening any hard lines or features. Furthermore, because the shape is so versatile, you can play with it to suit any face shape. If you have a hard jaw or a square face, curl the side pieces onto the face to soften the angularity. Dry this style with your fingers for nice natural movement. Curl it all over, or tong the edges, or pop in heated rollers – for a soft face-framing effect. For an unusual variation, put the back up in a French pleat and go on to curl the front using tongs or rollers.

Drying and styling

Finger-drying: You can put a lot of shape and bounce into short layered hair by lifting and drying with the fingers. Towel dry to blot up excess moisture. It is important to have your hair at the damp-dry stage before you begin finger-drying. If you begin when your hair is very wet, it will take much longer and the extra handling can mean that by the time your hair is dry it's also quite greasy.

Start off by simply running your fingers through your hair. Finger-drying is exactly the same technique as double brushing – but you are using your hands instead of brushes. Generally work in the direction in which you want the hair to go. For an off-the-face short, layered effect, work the hair away from the face all the time with upward movements, one hand following the other. And, on reaching the middle length and ends, keep turning the hands over to obtain a slightly curled effect at the ends.

Brush and blow drying: This is a quick and easy way of introducing shine and bounce into the hair. The secret is to

BELOW LEFT: *Finger-drying a short layered style, working the hair away from the face.*

BELOW RIGHT: *Brush and blow drying long hair, lifting the hair to speed the drying.*

have the hair at the damp-dry stage before you start. So after shampooing, comb all the tangles out of the hair, and blot dry with a towel. Ideally, leave your hair wrapped in the towel, turban-style, until you are ready to start blow drying.

The hair-do that blow dries most successfully of all is an absolutely perfect blunt cut. Your hand dryer shouldn't be too cumbersome to hold. Check that its speed is right for the effect you wish to achieve; a minimum of 900 watts is best for random blow drying.

With the brush in one hand, dryer in the other, concentrate on putting volume into the roots of the hair. Pull and stretch, section by section, and follow through the length of the hair, keeping the direction of the hot air going from root to end. Keep lifting the hair, to speed the drying process.

Or, as an alternative method, forget all about going along carefully, section by section. With your brush, wrap the hair around the head and brush round in the opposite direction to the final fall of the hair; this way you can coax a lot more volume into the roots.

Avoid over-drying your hair. When you reach the just-dry stage, run your hands through the hair. The slight amount of natural oil on your hands will help to prevent static building up and create a better shine.

Rollers and pin curl sets: Rollers come in all shapes and sizes. Use them to wet-set the hair or to dry-set it. If you are dry-setting, use heated rollers, lightweight plastic ones or the sponge variety. The size of rollers is important; those with a diameter of 3.5 cm ($1\frac{1}{2}$ inches), give a smooth effect and body to the hair. If your hair is limp or you want more curl, use smaller rollers. If you want your hair to wave rather than curl, twist each section of hair first and then wrap around the roller so that the hair unwinds in a spiral.

You will get the best results from a roller set if you part hair neatly and make each section no wider than the length of the roller and no deeper than the diameter of the roller. Comb each section of hair in the opposite direction from the way you will wind it: straight up for rollers that turn down at sides and back, straight forward for rollers that turn back over the top and crown.

Make sure the ends of your hair are smooth and flat against the roller before you wind it; if the very ends get hooked up, like a crochet hook, the final result is an uneven hairline. One

BELOW: *Dry-setting medium length hair. Large light rollers are used to achieve a flattering soft wavy style. Smaller ones are used at the sides – to obtain more curl.*

way to avoid this, especially with heated rollers, is to wrap a tissue round the roller, before placing it in your hair. Fasten each roller directly over the part of your scalp the hair wound around it grows. Fasten rollers securely so they won't sag as your hair dries. You might try clipping each roller to the one below. For added body, apply a little hair spray.

If you are wet-setting your hair, dry off excess moisture before putting in rollers. If possible, let your hair dry naturally, or use a hooded hairdryer. Do not try to speed up drying by holding a dryer too close to your head.

How to turn a pin curl: Pin curls make pretty fluffs of curls. Just as rollers placed in dry hair give a 'booster' set, so pin curls can put more spring into wispy tendrils around the hairline, on the forehead and at the sides of the face. When used to set wet hair, pin curls make really resilient curls. They will also set wisps of hair too short to go round rollers. And they can add body to a roller set when a single row is used above and behind the ears at the nape of the neck.

To make a perfect pin curl, take your section of hair, pop a tiny piece of cotton wool on the ends to keep them smooth and, starting at the centre of the strand, wind the end around your finger. Slide the coiled curl off your finger and turn in towards your scalp. Fasten with a pin curl clip.

BELOW*: For a professional pin-curl style take time to wind pincurls correctly. The secret is to wind in every stray hair before pinning.*

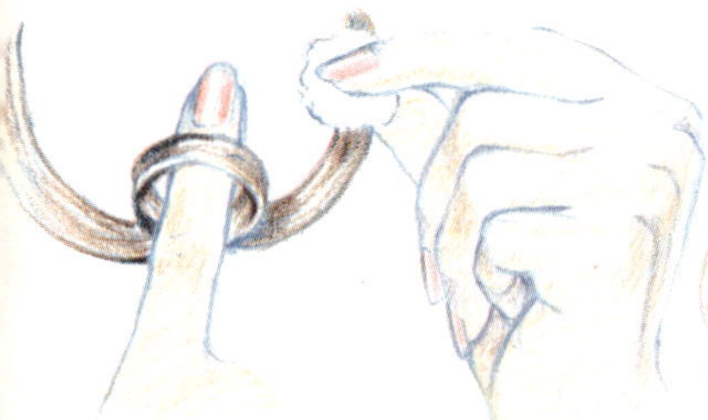

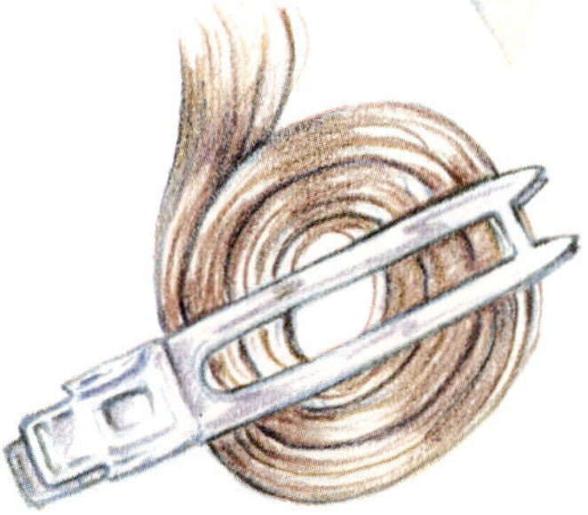

Curling tongs: These are suitable for any length of hair, whatever the style. They are used for adding fullness to the hair, curling and straightening, or for creating waves. Tongs are used mainly for adding a little more movement to your set immediately after blow drying; or for boosting a set in between shampoos – they are especially useful if you have greasy hair which 'drops' its set from one day to the next.

The basic technique is to part the hair into sections that are no more than 5 cm (2 inches) square, and to work on one section at a time. To prevent the ends of the hair from buckling, carefully wrap a tissue round them before you start to tong.

To coax maximum fullness and volume into the hair: Wind the whole head of hair in towards the scalp, section by section; leave in rolls all over the head until the hair has cooled down. By the time you finish rolling the last section the first will have cooled. Don't be tempted to brush or comb out your hair too quickly; you could finish with a frizzy style instead of beautifully shiny and controllable bounce.

To curl hair under: Start with the hair underneath. To do this, you should ideally pin the bulk of the hair out of the way; gradually unpinning it section by section. Start at the roots and smooth each section in the tongs; as you get towards the ends, curl the hair slightly. Do not 'roll' the entire length of the hair.

To wave hair: Place the tongs near the roots of each section. Then wrap the hair around the tongs, winding right to the very ends. Hold for 30 seconds. Unwind and leave in a ringlet to cool down. When you are waving with tongs, it is especially important to be careful about sectioning off the head tidily; this way you can get as near to the roots as you should. With haphazard and careless sectioning off, you will end up with 'sausage curls' starting half-way down the section of hair, instead of ringlets which spring from the scalp and comb out into waves that are full of movement and resilience. Unless you wind from the roots, the tongs can leave an imprint on the hair – where the movement starts – making it obvious that your waves are anything but natural.

If you intend to use curling tongs regularly, it is a good idea to apply an after-shampoo protein conditioner, as a preventative, just in case over-enthusiastic tonging has a drying effect on your hair.

ABOVE RIGHT: *Curling hair under, starting at the roots and smoothing down the length of each section.*

BELOW RIGHT: *Waving hair, wrapping each section round the tongs and winding right to the ends.*

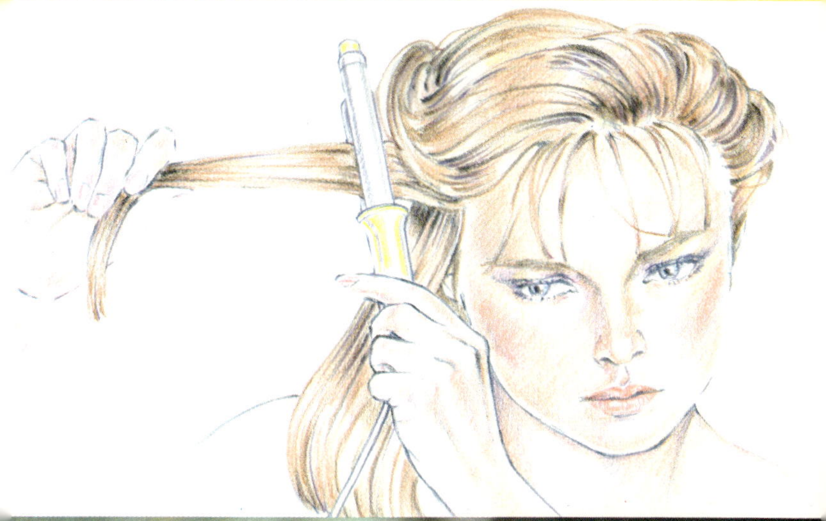

ABOVE: *Help with hennaring. A friend, wearing protective gloves, applies the henna to the hair section by section.*

Colouring and perming

Many hands make light work of perming or hair colouring. The problems of coping alone with a home perm or a hair colourant are twofold. In the first place, you can't see your head from every angle, even with a three-sided mirror. Secondly, just think how your arms ache if you have to hold them over your head for any length of time. So it definitely helps to have someone else carrying out the instructions for you. This is especially true with a home perm, as you can't wind the rollers properly at the back of the head yourself; also with a hair colourant which is applied to the hair section by section – it's impossible to make really regular partings in your own scalp. Help with the hennaring process is most valuable because it is rather a messy procedure. Henna is a natural vegetable dye from the dried leaves of an Egyptian privet. It comes in a powder form, which is mixed with boiling water to a paste – resembling green mud.

For real success with hair colour, narrow down the vast selection of shades available to those that suit your skin tone. Nature usually gives us complementary hair and face tones, but the match is very often low-key. Altering your hair shade simply intensifies the colour scheme and makes it high key.

The secret is to choose a colour that is no more than three shades darker than your natural colour and no more than four shades lighter. So if you are naturally blonde, you can lighten to ash tones or darken to really warm golden and honey shades. If you are naturally mousey, you can lighten to blonde or darken to rich honey, tawny brown or subdued-red. If you are naturally a redhead, you can lighten to a honey blonde shade – never an ash one – or darken to browny-chestnut or reddish-copper. If you are naturally dark brown, you can lighten to golden brown or honey blonde or deepen your colour to include glowing red highlights. If you are naturally grey, you can lighten to a pretty, highlighted grey or darken to a natural-looking brown.

How long will the colour last? As long as you want it to. Shampoo-in colourants vary from permanent and semi-permanent tints to temporary colourings which last from one shampoo to the next (and the next shampoo could be within a matter of hours if for some reason you don't like the effect). Henna is becoming more and more popular for anyone wanting colour and improved condition for their hair. Whichever method of hair colouring you choose, it's important to follow instructions to the letter – and that includes patch testing for possible allergy.

Perming is a much-maligned process simply because, in the old days, so much could – and often did – go wrong. But today's perms are designed to give special body to the hair and styling flexibility without odour or the fear of frizzing. Perming works by softening the structure of the hair and rearranging it in a curved or curled pattern. It's the way you wind the curl that sets the pattern of your perm. This is why it definitely helps to have a friend on hand to check that the hair is divided into neat sections and that the tissue-covered ends of each strand are wound neatly around the perm roller; a neutralizing agent then sets the hair in its new shape.

The technique for straightening hair is much the same as the process for perming it – but in reverse. A similar process is used, but the hair is straightened – rather than curled.

Diet & Exercise

Diet and exercise go hand in hand. Exercise helps burn up surplus fat; it also boosts circulation, keeps muscles toned and keeps joints supple. Exercise also nourishes the skin with extra oxygen from the blood stream, so improving the appearance of complexion and hair. For many people who have difficulty sleeping, physical activity helps considerably.

Literally everyone – fat, thin or just right – needs to take exercise. Only a few activities, like swimming, netball and fencing, tone all the muscles, but brisk exercise taken out-of-doors whenever possible is a good way of keeping you fit. A daily indoor session of ten minutes or so takes care of any muscles you may have missed while walking, jogging, cycling, bowling, etc.

A healthy approach to eating should – like exercise – become a way of life. The ideal daily diet should provide an adequate intake of all the essential nutrients for optimum health and vitality. It should be high in proteins, vitamins, minerals and essential oils but controlled in calories. To restrict calorie intake cut down on sugar, preserves, confectionery, cakes, biscuits and chips – foods which contain little else in the way of nutrients other than carbohydrate and are therefore called 'empty calories'. Foods which provide bulk to the system are much better for you, especially fruits, vegetables and nuts. These help to satisfy the appetite and provide valuable dietary fibre to aid digestion, but they are not concentrated sources of calories.

Being fat or thin is largely a question of metabolism – the process by which our intake of food is burnt up in the body. Two people may eat the same food and one may be fat, the other thin. It depends on the individual's metabolic rate; i.e. how much food he or she burns up during each day. There is nothing magical about slimming. If you eat less food than your body burns up, you will lose weight. If you consume more than your body needs, you will put on weight. If you are overweight, you must reduce your calorie intake, to encourage your body to use up excess fat reserves, which represent stored-up calories.

If you simply cut down on your normal intake of food in order to lose weight, you will be cutting down on your intake of vitamins, minerals and proteins too. When slimming it is most important to follow a diet rich in these vital nutrients in order to keep healthy.

Healthy Eating

To ensure that you are eating a healthy diet, it helps to recognise the essential nutrients your body requires. Everyone needs adequate protein, vitamins, minerals and energy to keep healthy. The chart below identifies the main sources of these nutrients, their functions in the body and deficiency symptoms.

Nutrient and Main Sources:	**Gives you:**	**Deficiency Symptoms:**
PROTEINS		
Animal proteins: meat, fish, eggs, milk, cheese. *Plant proteins*: cereals, pulses, nuts, bread.	Strong muscles, healthy skin; antibodies to fight disease.	Retarded growth in children. Susceptibility to infections and disease.
FATS		
Butter*, margarine, vegetable oils, lard*, fat in meat*, cream*, cheese*, milk*.	Energy for activity and warmth; some supply Vitamins A & D.	Lack of energy. Poor skin (*see Vitamins*).
CARBOHYDRATES		
Starches: Bread, cereals, pasta, rice, potatoes. Sugars: All types of sugar, honey, jam, dried fruit.	Energy. Most sugar carbohydrates provide quick energy but little else. Starches provide energy plus protein, minerals and B Vitamins.	Reduced stamina and energy.
VITAMINS		
Vitamin A: Liver, fats, carrots, spinach.	Healthy skin, hair, nails and eyes.	Eye, respiratory and skin problems.
Vitamin B Grp: Yeast extract, cereals, liver.	Essential links in metabolic processes.	Fatigue, depression.
Vitamin C: Citrus fruits, blackcurrants, cabbage, sprouts.	Resistance to infection; concerned with growth and repairing tissues.	Low resistance to infection, slow healing.
Vitamin D: Oily fish, liver, eggs, milk, butter, margarine.	Healthy bones and teeth.	Dental caries, rickets in children.
MINERALS		
Iron: liver, kidneys, beef, eggs, green vegetables.	Essential oxygen carrier in the blood.	Fatigue, anaemia.
Calcium: milk, cheese, sardines, bread.	Strong bones and teeth. Proper muscle and blood functioning.	Unhealthy teeth and bones.
Sodium: salt, bacon, ham, salt water fish.	Maintaining normal body fluid balance.	Muscular cramps.

The simplest way of obtaining enough of the necessary nutrients is to make sure meals are varied. Foods can be allocated to different groups, based on the nutrients they contain. Two average portions of food from each group every day should provide you with enough of all these nutrients.

Group 1 Meat, poultry, fish, eggs
Group 2 Milk, cheese, yogurt
Group 3 Fruit, vegetables
Group 4 Bread, pasta, cereals
Group 5 Butter, margarine, oils

Three meals a day – breakfast, one main meal and one light meal – should be sufficient to provide a healthy, balanced diet, but remember that every person's needs are slightly different, especially as far as calorie intake is concerned. It is also important to realise that most foods in groups 1 and 2 are also sources of fats (Group 5) – weight-watchers take note!

Vegetarians, particularly those who do not eat foods in either groups 1 or 2, should include a wide variety of vegetable (plant) protein foods instead; pulses – lentils, kidney beans, haricot beans, chick peas, etc – nuts and cereals are particularly good sources of vegetable protein. They also contain useful vitamins and minerals.

Recipe for beauty

The healthiest hair, the clearest eyes and the smoothest skin are as dependent on menus as make-up. Swinging, shiny hair and soft, supple skin depend on a good supply of protein and the A, B and C Vitamins; long, strong nails are an added plus. Milk, eggs, fish, citrus fruits and salads all contribute to these beauty assets. Vitamins A and B, contained in carrots, macaroni, wholemeal bread and cereal, promote healthy, clear eyes.

Every child relies on daily calcium to build up strong, straight bones and teeth. If the diet does not contain enough calcium, bones may not develop properly. The same thing can happen to the foetus during pregnancy if the mother does not eat enough calcium-rich foods. These include milk, cottage cheese, hard cheeses and yogurt.

Protein strengthens muscles and blood and is required for building up anti-bodies to fight disease. Vitamin C is essential for health and provides some degree of protection against colds and other infection. It also aids recovery from illness. Iron is vital for blood functioning; a deficiency in the diet can lead to fatigue and anaemia. Foods rich in iron are liver, kidney, beef, eggs and green vegetables.

When all teeth are fully developed 'diet rules' still apply to keep them healthy. Eat hard foods which necessitate chewing and plenty of cleansing foods which scour the teeth and stimulate the gums; apples, pears, celery, salad foods and hard crusts, for example. For healthy gums, take lots of Vitamin C foods – citrus fruits, rose-hip syrup, blackcurrants, lightly cooked green vegetables, salads, tomatoes and green peppers. Foods which are bad for teeth are soft sticky ones, especially sweets, cakes and synthetic fruit drinks containing a high proportion of sugar.

Beauty and health are inseparable. The younger you are when you appreciate this bond, the better. Long before a girl is thinking about make-up, she should be guided to eat properly. A healthy body, with strong bones and teeth, clear eyes and smooth skin is essential for beauty.

Enemies of beauty

Diet can help alleviate many of the complaints which visibly sap our looks and our vitality. Here are some of the more common complaints which can be helped by eating wisely.

Cellulite: This is a special type of obesity. Fat accumulates in stubborn globules, in areas such as the hips and thighs. The signs are unmistakeable: cellulite thickens the curves and the skin has a 'quilted' appearance. If you detect signs of cellulite, try to avoid foods which make toxins because these aggravate the condition. In this category are fatty meats, like pork and duck; rich butter or creamy sauces; fried foods; alcohol; strong cheeses; spicy foods and condiments; confectionery; tea and coffee.

Constipation: The outward signs are tired, cloudy-looking eyes, dull hair, clogged pores – especially on the chin, a furred tongue, clouded breath and a protruding stomach. Constipation can be caused by any of the following: eating plentifully but all the wrong foods, irregular meals, inadequate fluid intake. To avoid becoming constipated, make sure you are getting enough dietary fibre. Choose wholewheat bread and flour, and brown rice, in preference to their refined equivalents. Eat plenty of protein foods, lightly cooked vegetables, salads and fruit too.

One of the best ways of avoiding constipation is to take a bran cereal for breakfast; try eating a few soaked prunes or dried figs with, or instead of, the cereal. Also make sure that you are taking enough Vitamin B foods. Half a cupful of wheatgerm taken each day, cooked or uncooked, will often cure constipation. Even drinking more water may solve the problem; try drinking five glasses a day between meals if you are constipated.

Fluid retention: Pregnant women are liable to fluid retention or oedema as it is termed medically. This retention causes swelling, especially in the ankles, feet and hands. Most of us experience slight, not usually discernible, fluid retention just prior to the monthly period. Both types of fluid retention are due to the influence of hormones which are at a higher level at these times. For pregnancy the usual treatment is a high-protein, low-calorie, low-salt diet and rest. The monthly condition rights itself; there is no need to restrict fluid or salt. Once menstruation starts, any surplus fluid disappears and the bloated feeling subsides. If it does seem to be a permanent problem, however, don't simply reduce your fluid intake; consult your doctor.

Fluid retention must not be confused with ordinary weight gain, caused by over-eating. Heavy thighs, arms or ankles are much more likely to indicate fat retention than fluid retention and a good diet – coupled with plenty of exercise – will solve the problem.

Insomnia: A sound night's sleep is a necessity for beauty. Most adults need between seven and eight hours sleep each night and an extra bonus of sleep will often improve the looks as much as a holiday. When eyes are tired, the complexion is drab and spirits tend to be low; the cure can often be found in extra sleep.

If you sleep badly, check for constipation or indigestion. It is said that insomnia is often due to mild indigestion caused by a heavy, or indigestible, meal taken too near bedtime. Try making the last meal of the day light and digestible. Avoid tea or coffee late at night; have a milky drink or a cup of mint tea instead. Inability to sleep properly may also be a sign that you are not taking enough exercise during the day; take a brisk walk or a jog before sleeping – if you feel the need for a breath of fresh air. Alternatively, follow the 10-minute general exercise plan (see page 88). If you feel too alert or tense to sleep, try a simple relaxation routine (see page 92).

Migraine: A variety of factors have been suggested as trigger mechanisms for migraine attacks. Many of these are of stress origin, but some implicate certain foods, such as cheese, chocolate, wine (especially red), yeast extract and bananas. Too much fat, in any form, may also be a causative factor, so if you suffer from migraine, use less butter and avoid fried foods as much as possible.

Tension: A deficiency of thiamin (Vitamin B1) can lead to tension. Thiamin is found in whole grains, sunflower seeds, millet, chicken, fish roes, sardines, cod, lean beef, lean mutton, liver, pork, kidneys and brains.

Indoor fitness routine
For really effortless exercising, get yourself organized from the start. The ideal 'gym' is a well-ventilated, heated room. A full-length mirror enables you to check that your shoulders and face do not tense up. Exercise in clothing which does not restrict. The ideal 'flooring' is a rug or folded blanket, which help prevent bruising and skin irritations. If music helps you exercise, and relax, choose something with an even tempo.
Warming up: Here are two exercises to start your fitness routine. Warming up increases the circulation and gets the body ready for action. Without these preliminaries, you can put unnecessary strain on muscles and feel stiff afterwards.

1. Touch toes: *a) Stand tall, feet slightly apart and hands over head. b) Bend from waist to touch toes; knees straight. c) Return to starting position. Continue for 1 minute. Repeat at least 5 times; work up to 40.*

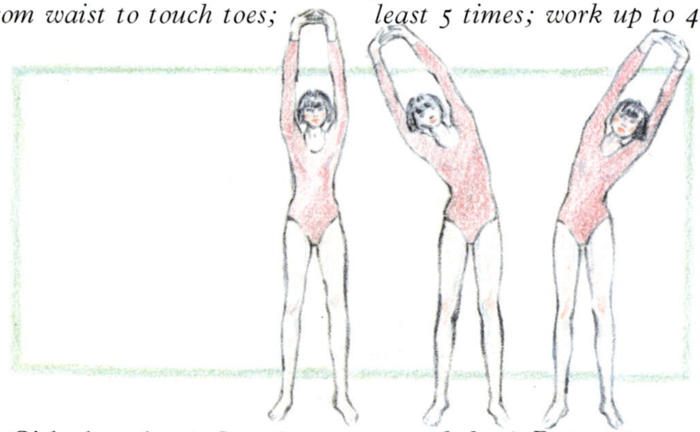

2. Side bend: *a) Stand tall, feet 12 inches apart and hands clasped above head. b) Bend to the right, keeping back straight and arms extended. c) Return to starting position and bend to left. Continue for 1 minute. Repeat at least 5 times each side; work up to 20.*

10-minute general exercise plan
This is a co-ordinated programme of movements designed to compensate for the general lack of physical activity and bodily movement in modern life. Follow the plan exactly, doing the exercises in the order listed and don't skip any. The exercises are designed to complement each other and tone muscles in all parts of the body – arms, legs, tummy, back etc. Begin with the two warm-ups (on pages 86–7), then proceed with the following eight exercises.

Do this routine every day – before breakfast is a good time. Run through the exercises again in the evening if you are not too tired. Never spend more than 1 minute on each exercise. As you get fitter, speed up your exercising to increase the number of exercises you do in 1 minute.

3. Squat: *a) Stand tall, feet together and arms extended. Rise on toes. b) Bend knees and, keeping back straight and arms extended, squat as low as you can. c) Slowly return to starting position. Begin with 10; go up to 15.*

4. Arm manoeuvre: *a) Stand tall, feet together and arms out in front – with hands above waist. b) Swing arms high, as far back as possible, keeping them stretched. c) Hold for a moment and swing back to starting position. Begin with 25 and speed up to 40.*

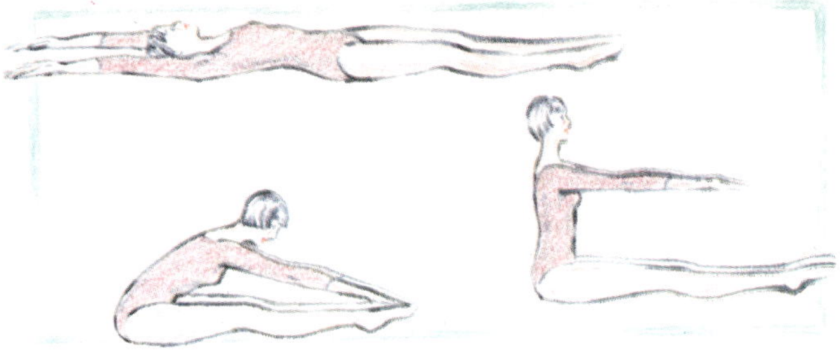

5. **Sit up:** *a) Lie flat, legs together and arms extended over head. b) Keeping legs still, and back as straight as possible, move to a sitting position. c) Now bend forwards from the waist to touch toes. Return to starting position. Begin with 10 and speed up to 20.*

6. **Leg swing:** *a) Stand tall, feet together, left hand against wall and right hand at side. b) Keeping back and legs straight and toes pointed, swing right leg as high as possible. c) Swing down and back. Exercise 10 times this side, 10 times right side. Speed up to 16 each side.*

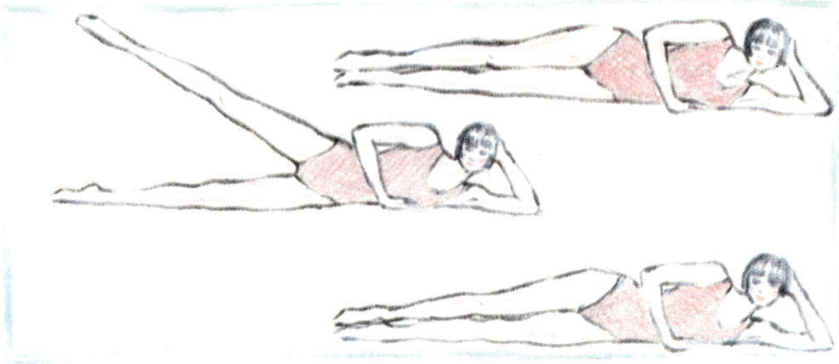

7. **Leg split:** *a) Lie on left side, legs straight, head resting on left arm, and right hand balancing on floor, in front at waist level. b) Keep legs straight, raise right one until it is 45° from floor. c) Return to first position. Begin with 10 for each leg. Speed up to 16.*

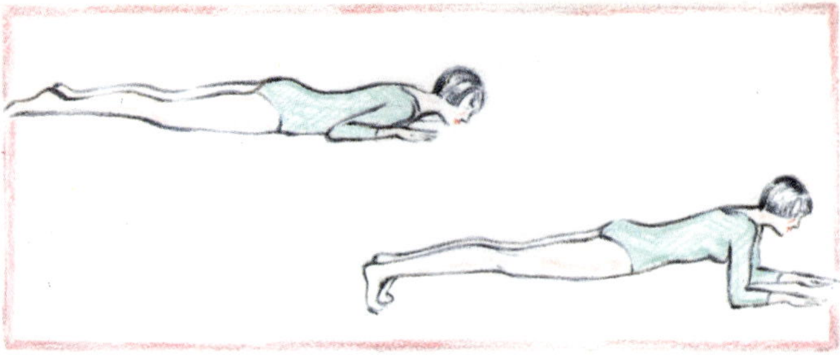

8. Push up: *a) Lie flat on your front, legs together, arms on floor and elbows in direct line with shoulders. b) By straightening back, raise body from floor and balance on toes and elbows. Lower body. Begin with 5; speed up to 10.*

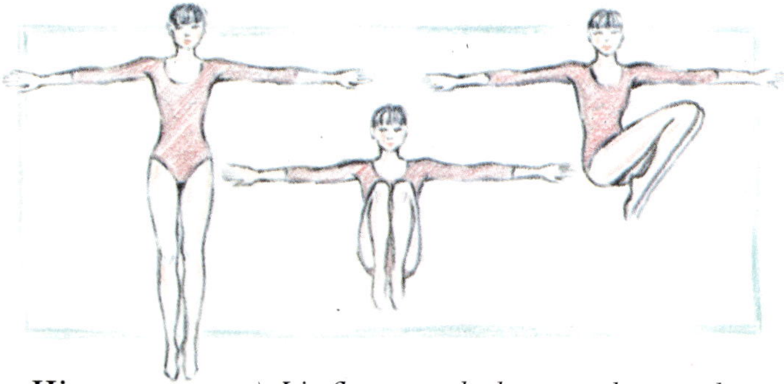

9. Hip squeeze: *a) Lie flat on your back, legs together, arms extended at shoulder level and palms down. Concentrate on keeping shoulders against floor. b) Keeping legs together, tuck them up close to chest. c) Roll over to left until left leg is flat on floor, keeping legs tucked up. Roll back until right leg is flat on floor. Begin with 10 and speed up to 20.*

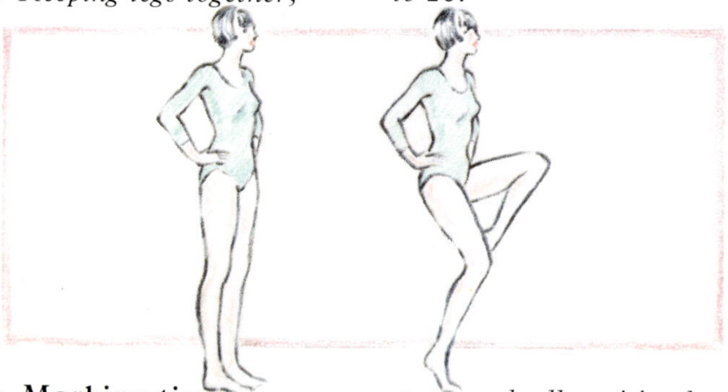

10. Marking time: *a) Stand tall, feet close together, shoulders back and hands on hips. Run on the spot, gradually raising knees higher and increasing speed. Do 100 beats, raising each knee 50 times. Go up to 150.*

Exercises like these can work miracles. It is possible to alter the shape of your body, though you cannot, of course, change the length of your bones. Remember there is no such thing as the ideal figure; perfect proportions are what matter. The scale of measurements to aim for is as follows: bust and hips should measure the same, waist should be 25 cm (10 inches) smaller than bust, thighs should be about 12 cm (6 inches) less than waist, calves about 12–15 cm (6–7 inches) less than thighs, ankles about 10 cm (5–6 inches) less than calves. Upper arms should be double the size of wrists.

Beauty bonuses

Breathing deeply, stimulates the brain and nervous system and helps the digestion of foods and liquids, by providing them with oxygen. It also purifies the lungs and, in turn, the blood, by carrying away toxins. Most of us get by on shallow breathing, but it's worth making a conscious effort to breathe deeply – especially in an effort to relax.

Deep breathing routine: Begin by doing each of the following breathing exercises three times and work up to six gradually. Sit on a chair or cross-legged on the floor. **1.** Place one hand on your chest and one on your diaphragm (midriff), then breathe from the top part of the lungs. This means that the hand placed on your chest should move, the diaphragm should hardly move at all. **2.** Consciously breathe from the diaphragm area. This time the hand on your chest should be still and the one on the diaphragm should move. **3.** Place both hands on your ribs and breathe so that the ribs and your hands move sideways. **4.** Place both hands on the sides of your ribcage and breathe so that the ribs seem to move backwards and sideways. **5.** This is the most difficult stage: Breathe in again, and this time completely, being aware of breathing from all 'compartments' in one breath. Hold your breath for a count of 5 and breathe out slowly.

How to relax

A simple relaxation routine encourages you to unwind completely – both mentally and physically. Do this whenever you can't sleep – either because you are too tense physically, or too alert mentally.

Ideally your bed should have a smooth, firm, level mattress and a resilient pillow. Your bedroom should be quiet, dark and airy. Even in ideal conditions, you may be unable to get to sleep if your mind is more tired than your body or vice versa. An imbalance, of this nature, between mind and body, can be put right by total relaxation.

If you are more mentally tired than physically tired, proceed with following the sequence of movements from toe-to-top, in the order given. In other words, let your flow of relaxation travel up slowly to the tension centre – the neck and beyond. But if you are more physically tired than mentally completely reverse the flow and work from top-to-toe.

Toes: Lying flat on your back, with feet slightly apart, stretch your big toes alternately, a few times, as if 'seeking' the end of the bed.

Ankles: Rotate each ankle, alternately and slowly, clockwise and anti-clockwise, then relax your feet leaving them totally limp.

Legs: Raise your legs, bent at knees and completely relaxed, letting the knees lean sideways and out. Remain in this position and count to thirty, then let your legs flop back on the mattress.

Bottom: Forgetting completely about your legs, put all your weight on your bottom. Clench and tighten the buttocks, as if you were trying to grip a coin between them, and pull in the tummy muscles at the same time. Count to ten, slacken, then count to ten again. Finally let everything go slack.

Back: Imagine that your spine is sinking into the depths of a really old-fashioned feather mattress. Let the softness encase you. If you still feel a few stubborn areas of tension in the small of the back, slide your thumbs up and let them massage the trouble spots.

Arms and hands: Raise arms slightly from the mattress. Open your fingers as wide as you can, as if you were stretching for an octave on the piano. Now suddenly let the arms drop, lifelessly. Repeat this movement about five times – until the arms feel quite limp and abandoned.

Shoulders and neck: Drop the shoulders as if you want to slide them further under the bedclothes. Now turn the head on the pillow to look to the right, to the left and the right again. Repeat once more.

Neck and jaw: Raise your head slightly from the pillow and stretch your neck to peer over the rim of the bedclothes. Repeat once or twice more. And suddenly you will find you don't want to take your head off the pillow.
Eyes: Keeping the head still, roll the eyes round to the right and to the left and to the right again. Repeat once more, then drift off to sleep!

A final word . . .
Now you should feel totally recharged from top-to-toe, and be tinglingly aware of every newly-awakened part of you. What matter that you don't measure up to perfection on every single beauty count? Work at the things you have been lax about, the potentially good points that have been lying dormant, or unexercised, or covered-up by an unflattering hairstyle. Work even harder at highlighting the assets – no matter how few you think they are – they are positive winners.

Once you are working away at the things you can see advantages in, the rest seems to fall into place. Hard work does bring its own rewards; the hitherto unmentionable defects fade into obscurity or out-of-all-recognition. One word of warning. Having discovered a whole new beautiful you, never rest on your laurels. Be aware of the never-ending sense of discovery you can enjoy; that's something unique to the beauty world. A change of make-up or hairstyle or even simply attitude to skin care, diet or exercise can bring a fresh new look.

Index